AFRICAN WRITERS SERIES

Editorial Adviser · Chinua Achebe

EQUIANO'S TRAVELS

THE

INTERESTING NARRATIVE

OF

THE LIFE

OF

OLAUDAH EQUIANO,

OR

GUSTAVUS VASSA,

THE AFRICAN.

WRITTEN BY HIMSELF.

VOL I.

Behold, God is my salvation; I will trust and not be afraid, for the Lord Jehovah is my strength and my song; he also is become my salvation.
And in that day shall ye say, Praise the Lord, call upon his name, declare his doings among the people. Isaiah xii. 2, 4.

LONDON:

Printed for and sold by the AUTHOR, No. 10, Union-Street, Middlesex Hospital;

Sold also by Mr. Johnson, St. Paul's Church-Yard; Mr. Murray, Fleet-Street; Messrs. Robson and Clark, Bond-Street; Mr. Davis, opposite Gray's Inn, Holborn; Messrs. Shepperson and Reynolds, and Mr. Jackson, Oxford-Street; Mr. Lackington, Chiswell-Street; Mr. Mathews, Strand; Mr. Murray, Prince's-Street, Soho; Mess. Taylor and Co. South Arch, Royal Exchange; Mr. Button, Newington-Causeway; Mr. Parsons, Paternoster-Row; and may be had of all the Booksellers in Town and Country.

[Entered at Stationer's Hall.]

Equiano's Travels

HIS AUTOBIOGRAPHY

*The Interesting Narrative of the Life of
Olaudah Equiano or Gustavus Vassa
the African*

Abridged and Edited by

PAUL EDWARDS

*Formerly Senior Lecturer, Department of English Literature,
University of Edinburgh*

HEINEMANN

Heinemann International Literature and Textbooks
a division of Heinemann Educational Books Ltd
Halley Court, Jordan Hill, Oxford OX2 8EJ

Heinemann : A Division of Reed Publishing (USA) Inc.,
361 Hanover Street, Portsmouth, New Hampshire, 03801-3912, USA

Heinemann Educational Books (Nigeria) Ltd
PMB 5205, Ibadan
Heinemann Educational Boleswa
PO Box 10103, Village Post Office, Gaborone, Botswana

LONDON   EDINBURGH   MELBOURNE   SYDNEY
AUCKLAND   SINGAPORE   TOKYO   PARIS
MADRID   ATHENS   BOLOGNA

ISBN 0 435 90010 2

*The Interesting Narrative of the Life of
Olaudah Equiano, or Gustavus Vassa the African,
Written by Himself,* first published 1789

Series Editor: Adewale Maja-Pearce

Printed and bound in Great Britain by
Cox & Wyman Ltd, Reading, Berkshire

93 94 95 96 12 11 10 9 8 7

Contents

List of Illustrations

frontis

The title page of the first edition of *The Interesting Narrative of the Life of Olaudah Equiano or Gustavus Vassa, the African*

View of Falmouth, 1806
(by R. Pollard after H. Michell, by courtesy of the National Maritime Museum)

View across Carlisle Bay to Bridge Town, Barbados
(from *Voyage to the West Indies* by J. A. Waller, 1820, by courtesy of the British Museum)

The Wreck of the Slave Ship *Nancy*
(from volume II of the original edition of *The Interesting Life*)

A Negro Dance Session
(from J. H. Parry and P. M. Sherlock *A Short History of the West Indies*, by courtesy of Macmillan & Co.)

A Spanish Planter of Porto Rico
(from *Voyage to the West Indies* by J. A. Waller, 1820, by courtesy of the British Museum)

The *Racehorse* and the *Carcass* in the Arctic, 1773
(from Phipps' *A Journal of a Voyage*, by courtesy of the British Museum)

Olaudah Equiano
(from the frontispiece of the original edition)

Phipps' Route to Spitsbergen
(a map from C. Phipps' *A Journal of a Voyage towards the North Pole, 1773* (London 1774), by courtesy of the British Museum)

PREFACE TO THE NEW IMPRESSION

A number of corrections and additions have been made to the first edition of the abridged text, in particular a manuscript letter of Equiano's which is printed here in Appendix III. A facsimile edition of the full text of Equiano's narrative is being published this year by Dawsons of Pall Mall in the Colonial History Series, where a rather more detailed discussion will be found in my introduction and notes, which have been extended from those in this volume.

EDITOR'S INTRODUCTION

Equiano's autobiography, *The Interesting Narrative of the Life of Olaudah Equiano, or Gustavus Vassa the African, written by himself*, was published in 1789, but in spite of its early date it was not the first work written by an African in English. The poems of Phyllis Wheatly appeared in 1773, Ignatius Sancho's collected letters in 1782, and Ottobah Cugoano's *Thoughts and Sentiments on the Evil and Wicked Traffic of Slavery* in 1787. But Equiano's book is of more lasting interest than any of these. Phyllis Wheatly's poems are commonplace exercises in the style of the period, and Sancho's letters, though lively in places, are often affected and obscure. These writers are not likely to interest the modern reader except as curiosities. The third writer, Cugoano, says little in his book about himself, and most of its pages are devoted to the denunciation of the slave trade, so that again its interest is for the historian or sociologist rather than the general public. In fact, it seems likely either that Cugoano did not write *Thoughts and Sentiments*, or that it was largely revised for him, for a letter exists in his own handwriting that reveals his style to lack the literary flourish displayed in his book.[1] It has been suggested that Equiano's autobiography, too, might have been 'improved' by another hand, and there is some evidence for revision since there appear to be two quite distinct styles in the book, the one plain, the other rhetorical. This question will be discussed later; but though there is always the possibility that the rhetorical passages may be revisions by another hand, the main part of the book is certainly Equiano's own, and in any case it is not the passages of the highest literary pretension which best display Equiano's narrative skill.

In its day *The Interesting Narrative* was something of a best seller, and it went through a large number of editions in Britain and America.[2] After the abolition of the slave trade, however, interest in it appears to have slackened; in fact, its early success must have been partly the result of Equiano's own efforts as he travelled through Britain making speeches against the slave trade and selling his book. The last edition to appear was an American one of 1837, and today, in Nigeria as elsewhere, Equiano's book is not well known except to historians. It has dated very little, however, and its chief attraction is still its lively, direct and observant narrative of travel and changing fortunes, likely to be enjoyed as much today as when it was written.

Equiano gives the date of his birth as 1745, and though this can only be an approximation it was probably accurate within a year or so.[3] He came from the interior of what is now Eastern Nigeria, and his language was Ibo. He tells us that he was born in 'a charming, fruitful vale called Essaka', and though this cannot be located with any certainty it seems to have been somewhere to the south-east of Onitsha. He says that his people were under the influence of Benin, though their 'subjection to the King of Benin was little more than nominal'. The influence of Benin on Onitsha and other towns on the Niger was considerable, and Benin's reputation extended much further than its direct power.[4]

At the age of ten he was captured with his sister by local raiders in search of slaves, and carried westwards and southwards until he reached a 'large river', where he was given over to a people who lived in boats and spoke a language different from his own. We should not expect a precise record of a journey made in childhood under such terrifying conditions, but it would be reasonable to assume that the river was probably the Niger or one of its tributaries, and the tribe speaking a different tongue one of the Delta peoples, perhaps Ijaw though the Ibibios were active in the northern part of the Delta at this time, and were boat-dwellers according to a late 18th-century account —see p. 183. After a journey down river with these people, he reached the sea, and was sold to slavers bound for the West Indies.

One of the earliest reviews of Equiano's book expressed doubts about the accuracy of his memories.[5] No doubt Equiano talked over his childhood with other Africans, and used this information in his book.[6] It seems likely, too, that some of his recollections were faulty, but complete accuracy could hardly be expected of him in the circumstances. The account he gives of Ibo society is generally very close to modern Ibo life, however, and where it differs we might allow for changing conditions as well as for inaccurate memories. It has been suggested that he was not an Ibo, but the few words he gives are recognizable as modern Ibo, particularly the word for 'year' (Ah-affoe, modern Ibo afɔ), and for men with ritual scars, (Embrenché, modern Ibo mgburichi). Names similar to Equiano can still be found in the probable region of Equiano's home: Chinua Achebe tells me that he knows of two people called ɛkwɛanɔ, which probably means 'if they agree I shall stay', a name implying someone unhappy with his companions. I have also been told of the name ɛkwuanθ meaning 'when they speak others attend', implying a member of a group of spokesmen. G. I. Jones, who believes Equiano to have come from the western bank of the Niger, refers to a common name amongst the Ika Ibo, Ekwuno.[7] Olaudah is more of a problem: but since he says that his name meant 'having a loud voice, and well spoken', the second element is likely to be modern Ibo θda, resonance. However, I have been told that the combination of ɔla (ornament) and udɛ (fame) could imply 'fortunate . . . one favoured'. But Ibo names are often difficult to interpret, even in modern times.

At this stage of his life, however, he lost his African name, being called first of all Michael, then Jacob, and finally, by his new master Lieutenant Pascal, Gustavus Vassa, the name he used for the rest of his life. In the years which followed his enslavement he travelled widely with Captain Pascal, serving him during the campaigns of General Wolfe in Canada, and Admiral Boscawen in the Mediterranean during the Seven Years War. He spent some time in England, staying at the homes of a number of English families and even receiving some schooling, which helped prepare him for his later work as a shipping clerk and amateur navigator on the ships of his second master, the Quaker Robert King of Philadelphia, travelling chiefly between America and the West Indies. On the whole he appears to have been more fortunate than most slaves in his masters. He found friends to help him with his education, such as Richard Baker ('Dick') who gave him his first English lessons, and the Misses Guerin, who sent him to school. He was even able to continue his education on board ship, for there was a school on board the *Namur* (p. 49); and on the *Aetna* (p. 56) the captain's clerk gave him lessons in writing and arithmetic. Even so, Lieutenant Pascal let him down badly by re-selling him when freedom had been promised, earned, and was expected: and even Mr King, who was probably under pressure to release all his slaves in accordance with Quaker belief, was very reluctant to do so in Equiano's case, only giving him freedom on payment of L.40 and on the urgent persuasion of Equiano's captain and friend, Thomas Farmer. Equiano was fortunate in being intelligent, quick to learn English, to write and to calculate, and it was probably this as much as any goodwill on the part of his masters that saved him from the worst horrors of slavery. But his own comparative good fortune we have to set against the glimpses he gives us of the common life of the West Indian slave. The fearful insecurity, not only of the slave but of the freed negro, is recorded constantly in such passages as the descriptions of the journey from Africa to the West Indies (pp. 25-32), the treatment of slaves (pp. 65-74), his first trading ventures (pp. 77-79) and his clash with the brutal Hughes (pp. 147-148).

After his release from slavery in 1766 at the age of twenty-one, the chief events of his life were his tour of the Mediterranean, his voyages to the Arctic and the Mosquito Shore of Central America, his conversion to Calvinism, and the part he played in the first expedition of freed slaves to settle in Sierra Leone in 1787. The last two are not included in any detail in these selections since they are of less interest to the general reader than the travels, but after the notes there is an appendix dealing with Equiano's appointment to and subsequent dismissal from the post of Commissary for Stores for the Black Poor going to Sierra Leone. On the whole, Equiano was probably in the right, and was most likely dismissed as a troublemaker because he was not prepared to turn a blind eye to corrupt procedures, and the neglect of the black settlers of which he accused other officers on the expedition. Though he was to have travelled to Sierra Leone, he got no further than Plymouth, where he was dismissed. Equiano's worst crime appears to have been his anxiety to see that justice was done to his own people, and there is ample testimony in his favour, though the strain of the delays at Plymouth, the sickness aboard ship, the growing uncertainty about prospects in Sierra Leone, and the negligence or dishonesty of the Agent, Irwin, may well have overburdened him.

Equiano had been in touch with the movement for the abolition of slavery, for some years before his book was published. In 1783, it was he who drew Granville Sharp's attention to the massacre of over 130 slaves aboard the *Zong* off the West African coast. Sharp recorded this note on 19 March: 'Gustavus Vassa, a negro, called on me, with an account of 130 negroes being thrown alive into the sea . . .'[8] and later wrote to the Admiralty demanding that some action be taken, 'having been earnestly solicited and called upon by a poor negro for my assistance to avenge the blood of his slaughtered countrymen'.[9] This case led to one of the many parliamentary battles over the slave trade, but it was many years before abolition became law, many years, in fact, after Equiano's death. But he persisted in his work against slavery. After his dismissal from his post in 1787 he completed his book and travelled through Britain selling copies and making speeches against the slave trade in a number of cities. Letters of recommendation from his friends show him visiting Birmingham in 1789, and Manchester, Sheffield and Nottingham in the following year. He was in Belfast on Christmas Day 1791, visited Durham and Hull in 1792, and was in the West of England, at Bath and Devizes, in 1793.[10] During these years he made enemies amongst those who stood to gain from the slave trade, and it seems to have been these who made charges against him in *The Oracle* of 25 April 1792 that he was not a native African, but was born on the Danish island of Santa Cruz in the West Indies. This story was repeated in *The Star* two days later. However, Equiano was able to produce evidence of his African origins, and the editor of *The Star* apologized, admitting that the story must have been a fabrication of the enemies of abolition, who would do anything to weaken the force of arguments against the slave trade.[11] After his visit to Birmingham in 1789, during which he appears to have been exceptionally well received, he wrote thanking his hosts:

> These acts of kindness and hospitality have filled me with a longing desire to see these worthy friends on my own estate in Africa, where the richest produce of it should be devoted to their entertainment. They should there partake of the luxuriant pineapples, and the well flavoured virgin palm-wine, and to heighten the bliss I would burn a certain tree, that would afford us light as clear and brilliant as the virtue of my guests.[12]

Equiano seems to have wanted very much to return to Africa, for in addition to his work for the 1787 expedition to Sierra Leone he volunteered to go as a missionary, his request being refused, and as an explorer for the African Association. But on 7 April 1792 he married a Miss Susan or Susanna Cullen. He may have met her through Dr Peter Peckard, Master of Magdalen College, Cambridge, and Dean of Peterborough, with whom he appears to have been on good terms. The marriage was noticed in *The Gentleman's Magazine*:

> At Soham, co. Cambridge, Gustavus Vassa the African, well known as the champion and advocate for procuring the

suppression of the slave trade, to Miss Cullen, daughter of Mr C. of Ely, in the same county.[13]

There is a record of his having a son, said by Henri Grégoire in his *De la Littérature des Nègres* to have been deputy librarian to the great book collector and President of the Royal Society, Sir Joseph Banks.[14] Since Grégoire's book was published in 1808, the son could hardly have been a child of this marriage, as he would have been at most fifteen years old on his appointment to the librarianship. The probable explanation has been suggested by Christopher Fyfe, who points out that a son of Ignatius Sancho, named William, did in fact work in Banks' library, and that Grégoire may have confused Sancho with Equiano.[15] This seems particularly likely since the short paragraph in which Grégoire mentions Equiano's son is in an isolated position at the end of the account of Equiano's life and immediately before that of Sancho. Short of saddling Equiano with an illegitimate child, we have to acknowledge that this son may have been conceived only in the imagination. There is evidence, however, that Equiano did have a daughter. A slip of paper inserted into a copy of Equiano's *Narrative* in the Royal Commonwealth Society Library in London has an inscription in a late 18th-century or early 19th-century hand, noting the death of 'Ann Maria Vassa, Daughter of Gustavus Vassa the African.' She is said to have died at the age of four on July 21st 1797, less than three months after her father.[16]

From the time at which the autobiography ends, comparatively little is known about Equiano's life. *The Gentleman's Magazine* records his death in London on 31 April 1797, but a few years later the editors of the 1809 (Belper) and the 1814 (Leeds) editions do not know the date of his death. The editor of 1809 gives it as 1801, and the editor of 1814 admits that he does not know. There is, however, one record of an eyewitness of Equiano's last moments. Granville Sharp's niece had been reading *The Interesting Narrative* and wrote to her uncle asking him about its author. Sharp wrote back to her 'He was a sober, honest man – and I went to see him when he lay upon his death bed, and had lost his voice so that he could only whisper . . .'[17]

At this point, something might be said briefly about the authorship of the book. From the first, some people have found it hard to believe that a former slave, and one who knew no English until he was twelve years old, could have written *The Interesting Narrative*. *The Monthly Review* of June 1789 praised the book, but felt 'it is not improbable that some English writer has assisted him in the compilement, or at least the correction of his book. for it is sufficiently well written'[18] That this happened in the case of Cugoano's *Thoughts and Sentiments* is very likely, but Cugoano's book is essentially very different from Equiano's. *Thoughts and Sentiments* is a work of abolitionist rhetoric, demanding a heightened style: *The Interesting Narrative* is largely a record of the ordinary circumstances of life, and the style, apart from the occasional excursion into protest and invocation, is appropriately plain and direct. Thus Equiano's book would have needed much less revision than Cugoano's, because of the nature of its subject and style. Again, we must remember that Equiano had received schooling even when a slave, had mixed constantly with Englishmen, and from the age of twenty-one had been a free man working as a valet, regularly in the company of educated people. There is no reason why he should not, at the age of forty-four, be perfectly fluent in English. Apart from one or two purple patches, in fact, Equiano's English is very plain, and occasionally even clumsy. *The Gentleman's Magazine* remarked on its 'very unequal style'[19] and another reviewer, in *The General Magazine and Impartial Review*, called it ' "a round unvarnished tale" . . . written with much truth and simplicity'.[20] Had the book been revised in any detail, we might have expected generally a much more elaborate style and certainly the removal of all awkward or ungrammatical expressions. In fact, these are not removed, and it is this simplicity and naturalness which gives the book much of its character and interest. If the book was revised, the revisions probably consisted of little more than the working up of occasional rhetorical climaxes. Striking evidence for Equiano's own hand is to be found in a poem which he prints immediately after his account of his conversion to Calvinism. [21] It is a fairly competent though dull piece of religious verse, and bears the un-

mistakable imprint of a West African author in its rhymes–
rhymes which are false unless spoken with a West African
English accent, and which can still be found in modern West
African verse. There is, for example, the merging of the long
and short [i] sounds, so that Equiano rhymes 'between-sin',
'relieve-give', 'sin-clean'. Other rhymes in the poem are less
distinctive, since they occasionally occur as eye rhymes, or plain
bad rhymes, in English verse of the period: but occurring as
they do with a cluster of distinctive West African rhymes, in a
poem supposedly written by a West African, they form further
strong evidence for its authenticity. There is the identification
of the long [i:] and the diphthong [ei] in 'been-pain', 'conceal-
prevail', and of the [u] or [u:] and the diphthong [ou] in 'do-
woe', 'good-showed', 'know-do'. And finally there are examples
of the confusion of the central vowel [ə:] and the vowel [ɔ:] in
'word-Lord' (though this is often found as an eye-rhyme in 18th-
century verse): and the confusion of [s] and [z], in 'please-
release'. If Equiano was capable of writing these verses himself,
there is no reason at all why he should not have written the
whole book.

But the most distinctive evidence of all is a manuscript letter
of Equiano's to be found in Appendix III of this volume. The
letter was written at great speed, as Equiano says himself
several times in the letter, and there are a few minor errors in it.
But not only are these errors fairly insignificant in this context
(they resemble errors made by British students writing at speed
in examinations); wherever an error of grammar occurs, at
some point in the letter the same grammatical form occurs
correctly, which indicates that haste, not ignorance of the
correct form, caused the mistake. Here, then, is decisive evidence
that Equiano was fluent and articulate in written English.[22]

Since Equiano made no claims to be a literary artist, it would
be unreasonable to make a serious comparison between him
and the major novelists of his time. All the same, the situation
of Equiano has something of Robinson Crusoe and something
too of Gulliver about it: it is a tale of economic and moral sur-
vival, like *Robinson Crusoe*, except that Equiano's desert island
is the world of slavery; and like Gulliver in Brobdingnag,

Equiano explores what it is like to find oneself suddenly phy-
sically alien in an incomprehensible world, and how the alien
individual gains his perspective in this world. Equiano has
many of the characteristics of the 18th-century literary hero
or narrator, emerging from his narrative as a wholly convincing,
living personality prepared to reveal the truth about himself
whether or not it is entirely pleasant. Sometimes we see him
at a loss, ignorant, confused and helpless: at others he shows
himself as self-seeking, and makes fun of his own weaknesses,
as in the episode on pp. 93-95 when he and Captain Farmer
are disappointed in their hopes of getting a small fortune from
a dying passenger. Twice within a few pages (pp. 130-133) he
nearly blows up his ship through carelessness, and the same
kind of comic self-revelation occurs in such incidents as those of
the grampuses (pp. 37-38) and the wild horseback ride (pp.
54-55). His feelings on the death of Captain Farmer are interest-
ingly ambivalent, caught as he is between affection for a friend
and pleasure at his release, not from an enemy but from a
benefactor, a striking demonstration of the psychology of
subordination. The death of Farmer releases him from a sense
of obligation and provides him with his first opportunity to act
out his new role of free man, significantly by steering the ship,
and it is worth noticing that in his next voyage he again takes
over the role of captain. The emancipation of the slave is brought
about not merely by the payment of forty pounds, but by his
acting out the roles of dominance through which he is able to
shed his past.

The language of the book, too, is often striking for unexpected reasons. At first sight it might be thought that the
heightened, rhetorical language of, for example, the end of the
'slave ship' chapter illustrates Equiano at his best. But the naive
language found earlier in the chapter, particularly on pp. 27-
28, is in fact handled with considerable subtlety and dramatic
skill. Notice that the näive terms—'this hollow place' for the
ship, 'cloth put upon the masts' for the sails, 'some spell or magic
they put upon the water to stop the vessel' for the anchor—all
these terms help to express the speaker's simplicity and puzzle-
ment: Equiano does not merely describe his perplexity, his

language becomes that of a perplexed boy. The same is true of the dialogue: notice the naive assumption behind 'how comes it in all our country we never heard of them?', the implied ignorance of the more 'knowledgeable' people who are answering the boy's questions, and the effect gained by the very simplicity of the question and response, itself suggesting an innocent, untutored view of life. Many of the best effects of Equiano's *Narrative* are in fact gained not by the lofty rhetoric, but by this kind of skilful dramatic simplicity. He never wholly loses his sense of proportion, tries to fight prejudice with reason, and makes no effort to capture our sympathies sentimentally by presenting himself as a man persistently ill-treated by an irredeemably wicked world. His white men are like his fortunes, a very realistically mixed bag. As a rule he puts no more emotional pressure on the reader than the situation itself contains – his language does not strain after our sympathy, but he expects it to be given naturally and at the proper time. This quiet avoidance of emotional display produces many of the best passages in the book.

Since this text is intended for the general reader as well as the student, a number of passages of limited interest have been excluded, but the selections have been arranged to form a consecutive narrative. Where a passage of any considerable length has been excluded, mention is made of this in the notes. A few unusual or archaic spellings have been given their modern form, (e.g. ankles for ancles, choose for chuse) and place names, too, have been modernised unless there is some reason for preserving the original spelling. Punctuation has been considerably lightened, in accordance with modern convention, since to keep the original punctuation would often confuse the reader.

Finally, I should like to thank Christopher Fyfe of Edinburgh University, the Ibo students of Fourah Bay College, Freetown, and Chinua Achebe for the help they have given so willingly; also the City of Liverpool Library, for permission to publish the letter in Appendix III, from the Hornby Collection, and Mr E. H. Seagroatt for drawing my attention to it.

Notes

[1] This is referred to by Christopher Fyfe, in his *History of Sierra Leone* (OUP 1962), p. 13. The letter is printed in the Appendix to a new edition of Cugoano's *Thoughts and Sentiments* (Dawsons 1969), along with four other manuscript letters. The introduction to this edition discusses the question of the authenticity of Cugoano's book in the light of these letters, and the occurrence of both a high proportion of grammatical errors and passages in eloquent and impeccable English, in Cugoano's book. It is worth remarking that there is some evidence of Equiano's hand in *Thoughts and Sentiments*. A report from the Africans on the Sierra Leone expedition of 1787 was sent up from Plymouth to Cugoano, and Cugoano passed it on to the *Public Advertiser*, which published a summary of it on April 6th 1787. This report was almost certainly the work of Equiano, who was the Africans' principal spokesman. Yet it contains a number of expressions later to be found on pp. 139-142 of Cugoano's book. There is no doubt that *Thoughts and Sentiments* must have been extensively revised, and it may be that Equiano, a close friend of Cugoano, was one of the revisers.

[2] There were eight British editions and one American published in Equiano's lifetime, and ten published posthumously, including translations into Dutch and German. For details, see the editor's introduction to the reprint of Equiano's *Interesting Narrative* in the Colonial Historical Series, published by Dawsons in 1969.

[3] see note on 'Six or seven months', p. 184.

[4] see K. Dike *Trade and Politics in the Niger Delta* (OUP 1956), p. 25.

[5] *Monthly Review*, June 1789, p. 551.

[6] He borrowed a paragraph from the life of James Albert Ukawsaw Gronniosaw, for example; see note on 'I had a great curiosity to talk to the books', p. 186.

[7] See G. I. Jones' introduction to passages from Equiano in Philip Curtin (ed.) *Africa Remembered* (University of Wisconsin Press 1967). In my introduction to the Colonial History Series edition of Equiano (Dawsons 1969), arguments are put forward

against Jones' case for a western location of Essaka.

[8] P. Hoare, *Memoir of Granville Sharp* (London 1820), p. 236.

[9] ibid., p. 242.

[10] Letters prefatory to the sixth edition of *The Interesting Narrative* (1793).

[11] ibid., pp. v–vi.

[12] J. A. Langford, *A Century of Birmingham Life* (1868), I. 440–41.

[13] *Gentleman's Magazine* (1792), Part I, p. 384. The entry of the marriage on 7 April 1792 – entry no. 220 – is recorded at Soham Church.

[14] H. Grégoire, *De La Littérature des Nègres* (Paris 1808), p. 252.

[15] A letter inserted into a copy of Sancho's letters owned by Mr Fyfe is marked 'From the son of Ignatius Sancho, who was for some years in the library of Sir Joseph Banks . . .' Details can be found in the editor's introduction to *The Letters of Ignatius Sancho* (Dawsons 1968).

[16] Details can be found in the editor's introduction to *The Interesting Narrative etc.* (Dawsons 1969).

[17] Granville Sharp papers at Hardwicke Court, Glos., Sharp to his niece Jemima on 22 February 1811.

[18] *Monthly Review*, June 1789, p. 551.

[19] *Gentleman's Magazine* (1789), p. 539.

[20] *General Magazine and Impartial Review*, July 1789.

[21] see Appendix II.

[22] For a discussion of this letter see Paul Edwards, '. . . *written by himself*': *A Manuscript Letter of Olaudah Equiano*, in *Notes and Queries* June 1968 pp. 222–225; or the editor's introduction to *The Interesting Narrative etc.* (Dawsons 1969).

View of Falmouth by R. Pollard

View across Carlisle Bay to Bridge
eighteenth

(after H. Michell) 1806

Town, Barbados at the end of the
century

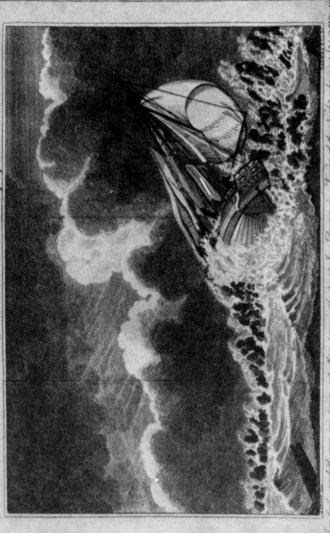

The Wreck of the Slave Ship *Nancy* on the Bahama Banks in 1767

A Negro dance session

A Spanish Planter of Porto Rico luxuriating in his hammock

View of the RACEHORSE and CARCASS, August 7th 1773.

J^n Cleveley Junr delin Mar 1st 1774.

Phipps' expedition: the *Racehorse* and the *Carcass* in the Arctic

Olaudah Equiano

CHAPTER ONE

My Early Life in Eboe

THAT part of Africa known by the name of Guinea to which the trade for slaves is carried on extends along the coast above 3,400 miles, from the Senegal to Angola, and includes a variety of kingdoms. Of these the most considerable is the kingdom of Benin, both as to extent and wealth, the richness and cultivation of the soil, the power of its king, and the number and warlike disposition of the inhabitants. It is situated nearly under the line and extends along the coast about 170 miles, but runs back into the interior part of Africa to a distance hitherto I believe unexplored by any traveller, and seems only terminated at length by the empire of Abyssinia, near 1,500 miles from its beginning. This kingdom is divided into many provinces or districts, in one of the most remote and fertile of which, called Eboe, I was born in the year 1745, situated in a charming fruitful vale, named Essaka. The distance of this province from the capital of Benin and the sea coast must be very considerable, for I had never heard of white men or Europeans, nor of the sea, and our subjection to the king of Benin was little more than nominal; for every transaction of the government, as far as my slender observation extended, was conducted by the chiefs or elders of the place. The manners and government of a people who have little commerce with other countries are generally very simple, and the history of what passes in one family or village may serve as a specimen of a nation. My father was one of those elders or chiefs I have spoken of and was styled Embrenché, a term as I remember importing the highest distinction, and signifying in our language a *mark* of grandeur. This mark is conferred on the person entitled to it by cutting the skin across at the top of the forehead and drawing it down to the eyebrows, and while it is in this situation applying a warm hand and rubbing it until it shrinks up into a thick *weal* across the lower part of the fore-head. Most of the judges and senators were thus marked; my father had long borne it. I had seen it conferred on one of my brothers, and I was also *destined* to receive it by my parents. Those Embrenché or chief men decided disputes and punished crimes, for which purpose they always assembled together. The proceedings were generally short, and in most cases the law of retaliation prevailed. I remember a man was brought before my father and the other judges for kidnapping a boy, and although he was the son of a chief or senator, he was condemned to make re-compense by a man or woman slave. Adultery, however, was sometimes punished with slavery or death, a punish-ment which I believe is inflicted on it throughout most of the nations of Africa, so sacred among them is the honour of the marriage bed and so jealous are they of the fidelity of their wives. Of this I recollect an instance – a woman was convicted before the judges of adultery, and delivered over, as the custom was, to her husband, to be punished. Accordingly he determined to put her to death: but it being found just before her execution that she had an infant at her breast, and no woman being prevailed on to perform the part of a nurse, she was spared on account of the child. The men however do not preserve the same constancy to their wives which they expect from them, for they indulge in a plurality, though seldom in more than two. Their mode of marriage is thus: both parties are usually betrothed when young by their parents, (though I have known the males to betroth themselves). On this occasion a feast is prepared, and the bride and bridegroom stand up in the midst of all their friends who are assembled for the purpose, while he declares she is thenceforth to be looked upon as his wife, and that no other person is to pay any addresses to her. This is also immediately proclaimed in the vicinity, on which the bride retires from the assembly. Some time after she is brought home to her husband, and then another feast is made to which the relations of both parties are invited: her parents then deliver her to the bridegroom accompanied with a number of blessings, and at the same time they tie round her waist a cotton string of the thickness of a goose-quill, which none but married women are permitted to wear: she is now considered as completely his wife, and at this time the dowry is given to the new married pair, which generally consists of portions of land, slaves, and cattle, household goods, and implements of husbandry. These are offered by the friends of both parties, besides which the parents of the bridegroom present gifts to those of the bride, whose property she is looked upon before marriage; but after it she is esteemed the sole property of her husband. The ceremony being now ended, the festival begins, which is celebrated with bonfires and loud acclamations of joy accompanied with music and dancing.

We are almost a nation of dancers, musicians, and poets. Thus every great event such as a triumphant return from battle or other cause of public rejoicing is celebrated in public dances, which are accompanied with songs and music suited to the occasion. The assembly is separated into four divisions, which dance either apart or in succession, and each with a character peculiar to itself. The first division contains the married men, who in their dances frequently exhibit feats of arms and the representation of a battle. To these succeed the married women, who dance in the second division. The young men occupy the third and the maidens the fourth. Each represents some interesting scene of real life, such as a great achievement, domestic employment, a pathetic story, or some rural sport, and as the subject is generally founded on some recent event it is therefore ever new. This gives our dances a spirit and variety which I have scarcely seen elsewhere. We have many musical instruments, particularly drums of different kinds, a piece of music which resembles a guitar, and another much like a stickado. These last are chiefly used by betrothed virgins who play on them on all grand festivals.

As our manners are simple, our luxuries are few. The dress of both sexes is nearly the same. It generally consists of a long piece of calico or muslin, wrapped loosely round the body somewhat in the form of a highland plaid. This is usually dyed blue, which is our favourite colour. It is extracted from a berry and is brighter and richer than any I have seen in Europe. Besides this our women of distinction wear golden ornaments, which they dispose with some profusion on their arms and legs. When our women are not employed with the men in tillage, their usual occupation is spinning and weaving cotton, which they afterwards dye and make into garments. They also manufacture earthen vessels, of which we have many kinds. Among the rest tobacco pipes, made after the same fashion and used in the same manner, as those in Turkey.

Our manner of living is entirely plain, for as yet the natives are unacquainted with those refinements in cookery which debauch the taste: bullocks, goats, and poultry, supply the greatest part of their food. These constitute likewise the principal wealth of the country and the chief articles of its commerce. The flesh is usually stewed in a pan; to make it savoury we sometimes use also pepper and other spices, and we have salt made of wood ashes. Our vegetables are mostly plantains, eadas, yams, beans, and Indian corn. The head of the family usually eats alone; his wives and slaves have also their separate tables. Before we taste food we always wash our hands: indeed our cleanliness on all occasions is extreme, but on this it is an indispensable ceremony. After washing, libation is made by pouring out a small portion of the drink on the floor, and tossing a small quantity of the food in a certain place for the spirits of departed relations, which the natives suppose to preside over their conduct and guard them from evil. They are totally unacquainted with strong or spirituous liquors, and their principal beverage is palm wine. This is got from a tree of that name by tapping it at the top and fastening a large gourd to it, and sometimes one tree will yield three or four gallons in a night. When just drawn it is of a most delicious sweetness, but in a few days it acquires a tartish and more spirituous flavour, though I never saw anyone intoxicated by it. The same tree also produces nuts and oil. Our principal luxury is in perfumes; one sort of these is an odoriferous wood of delicious fragrance, the other a kind of earth, a small portion of which thrown into the fire diffuses a more powerful odour. We beat this wood into powder and mix it with palm oil, with which both men and women perfume themselves.

In our buildings we study convenience rather than ornament. Each master of a family has a large square piece of ground, surrounded with a moat or fence or enclosed with a wall made of red earth tempered, which when dry is as hard as brick. Within this are his houses to accommodate his family and slaves which if numerous frequently present the appearance of a village. In the middle stands the principal building, appropriated to the sole use of the master and consisting of two apartments, in one of which he sits in the day with his family. The other is left apart for the reception of his friends. He has besides these a distinct apartment in which he sleeps, together with his male children. On each side are the apartments of his wives, who have also their separate day and night houses. The habitations of the slaves and their families are distributed throughout the rest of the enclosure. These houses never exceed one storey in height: they are always built of wood or stakes driven into the ground, crossed with wattles, and neatly plastered within and without. The roof is thatched with reeds. Our day-houses are left open at the sides, but those in which we sleep are always covered, and plastered in the inside with a composition mixed with cow-dung to keep off the different insects which annoy us during the night. The walls and floors also of these are generally covered with mats. Our beds consist of a platform raised three or four feet from the ground, on which are laid skins and different parts of a spungy tree called plantain. Our covering is calico or muslin, the same as our dress. The usual seats are a few logs of wood, but we have benches, which are generally perfumed to accommodate strangers: these compose the greater part of our household furniture. Houses so constructed and furnished require but little skill to erect them. Every man is a sufficient architect for the purpose. The whole neighbourhood afford their unanimous assistance in building them and in return receive and expect no other recompense than a feast.

As we live in a country where nature is prodigal of her favours, our wants are few and easily supplied; of course we have few manufactures. They consist for the most part of calicoes, earthenware, ornaments, and instruments of war and husbandry. But these make no part of our commerce, the principal articles of which, as I have observed, are provisions. In such a state money is of little use; however we have some small pieces of coin, if I may call them such. They are made something like an anchor, but I do not remember either their value or denomination. We have also markets, at which I have been frequently with my mother. These are sometimes visited by stout mahogany-coloured men from the south-west of us: we call them *Oye-Eboe*, which term signifies red men living at a distance. They generally bring us fire-arms, gunpowder, hats, beads, and dried fish. The last we esteemed a great rarity as our waters were only brooks and springs. These articles they barter with us for odoriferous woods and earth, and our salt of wood ashes. They always carry slaves through our land, but the strictest account is exacted of their manner of procuring them before they are suffered to pass. Some-times indeed we sold slaves to them, but they were only prisoners of war, or such among us as had been convicted of kidnapping, or adultery, and some other crimes which we esteemed heinous. This practice of kidnapping induces me to think that, notwithstanding all our strictness, their principal business among us was to trepan our people. I remember too they carried great sacks along with them, which not long after I had an opportunity of fatally seeing applied to that infamous purpose.

Our land is uncommonly rich and fruitful, and produces all kinds of vegetables in great abundance. We have plenty of Indian corn, and vast quantities of cotton and tobacco. Our pineapples grow without culture; they are about the size of the largest sugar-loaf and finely flavoured. We have also spices of different kinds, particularly pepper, and a variety of delicious fruits which I have never seen in Europe, together with gums of various kinds and honey in abundance. All our industry is exerted to improve those blessings of nature. Agriculture is our chief employment, and everyone, even the children and women, are engaged in it. Thus we are all habituated to labour from our earliest years. Everyone contributes something to the common stock, and as we are unacquainted with idleness we have no beggars. The benefits of such a mode of living are obvious. The West India planters prefer the slaves of Benin or Eboe to those of any other part of Guinea for their hardiness, intelligence, integrity, and zeal. Those benefits are felt by us in the general healthiness of the people, and in their vigour and activity; I might have added too in their comeliness. Deformity is indeed unknown amongst us, I mean that of shape. Numbers of the natives of Eboe now in London might be brought in support of this assertion, for in regard to complexion, ideas of beauty are wholly relative. I remember while in Africa to have seen three negro children who were tawny, and another quite white, who were universally regarded by myself and the natives in general, as far as related to their complexions, as deformed. Our women too were in my eyes at least uncommonly graceful, alert, and modest to a degree of bashfulness; nor do I remember to have ever heard of an instance of incontinence amongst them before marriage. They are also remarkably cheerful. Indeed cheerfulness and affability are two of the leading characteristics of our nation.

Our tillage is exercised in a large plain or common, some hours walk from our dwellings, and all the neighbours resort thither in a body. They use no beasts of husbandry, and their only instruments are hoes, axes, shovels, and beaks, or pointed iron to dig with. Sometimes we are visited by locusts, which come in large clouds so as to darken the air and destroy our harvest. This however happens rarely, but when it does a famine is produced by it. I remember an instance or two wherein this happened. This common is often the theatre of war, and therefore when our people go out to till their land they not only go in a body but generally take their arms with them for fear of a surprise, and when they apprehend an invasion they guard the avenues to their dwellings by driving sticks into the ground, which are so sharp at one end as to pierce the foot and are generally dipped in poison. From what I can recollect of these battles, they appear to have been irruptions of one little state or district on the other to obtain prisoners or booty. Perhaps they were incited to this by those traders who brought the European goods I mentioned amongst us. Such a mode of obtaining slaves in Africa is common, and I believe more are procured this way and by kidnapping than any other. When a trader wants slaves he applies to a chief for them and tempts him with his wares. It is not extraordinary if on this occasion he yields to the temptation with as little firmness, and accepts the price of his fellow creatures liberty with as little reluctance as the enlightened merchant. Accordingly he falls on his neighbours and a desperate battle ensues. If he prevails and takes prisoners, he gratifies his avarice by selling them; but if his party be vanquished and he falls into the hands of the enemy, he is put to death: for as he has been known to foment their quarrels it is thought dangerous to let him survive, and no ransom can save him, though all other prisoners may be redeemed. We have fire-arms, bows and arrows, broad two-edged swords and javelins: we have shields also which cover a man from head to foot. All are taught the use of these weapons; even our women are warriors and march boldly out to fight along with the men. Our whole district is a kind of militia: on a certain signal given, such as the firing of a gun at night, they all rise in arms and rush upon their enemy. It is perhaps something remarkable that when our people march to the field a red flag or banner is borne before them. I was once a witness to a battle in our common. We had been all at work in it one day as usual, when our people were suddenly attacked. I climbed a tree at some distance, from which I beheld the fight. There were many women as well as men on both sides; among others my mother was there, and armed with a broad sword. After fighting for a considerable time with great fury and after many had been killed, our people obtained the victory and took their enemy's Chief prisoner. He was carried off in great triumph, and though he offered a large ransom for his life he was put to death. A virgin of note among our enemies had been slain in the battle, and her arm was exposed in our market-place where our trophies were always exhibited. The spoils were divided according to the merit of the warriors. Those prisoners which were not sold or redeemed we kept as slaves: but how different was their condition from that of the slaves in the West Indies! With us they do no more work than other members of the community, even their master; their food, clothing and lodging were nearly the same as theirs, (except that they were not permitted to eat with those who were free-born), and there was scarce any other difference between them than a superior degree of importance which the head of a family possesses in our state, and that authority which, as such, he exercises over every part of his household. Some of these slaves have even slaves under them as their own property and for their own use.

As to religion, the natives believe that there is one Creator of all things and that he lives in the sun and is girded round with a belt that he may never eat or drink; but according to some he smokes a pipe, which is our own favourite luxury. They believe he governs events, especially our deaths or captivity, but as for the doctrine of eternity, I do not remember to have ever heard of it: some however believe in the transmigration of souls in a certain degree. Those spirits which are not transmigrated, such as their dear friends or relations, they believe always attend them and guard them from the bad spirits or their foes. For this reason they always before eating, as I have observed, put some small portion of the meat and pour some of their drink, on the ground for them, and they often make oblations of the blood of beasts or fowls at their graves. I was very fond of my mother and almost constantly with her. When she went to make these oblations at her mother's tomb, which was a kind of small solitary thatched house, I sometimes attended her. There she made her libations and spent most of the night in cries and lamentations. I have been often extremely terrified on these occasions. The loneliness of the place, the darkness of the night, and the ceremony of libation, naturally awful and gloomy, were heightened by my mother's lamentations; and these, concurring with the doleful cries of birds by which these places were frequented, gave an inexpressible terror to the scene.

We compute the year from the day on which the sun crosses the line, and on its setting that evening there is a general shout throughout the land; at least I can speak from my own knowledge throughout our vicinity. The people at the same time make a great noise with rattles, not unlike the basket rattles used by children here, though much larger, and hold up their hands to heaven for a blessing. It is then the greatest offerings are made, and those children whom our wise men foretell will be fortunate are then presented to different people. I remember many used to come to see me, and I was carried about to others for that purpose. They have many offerings, particularly at full moons; generally two at harvest before the fruits are taken out of the ground, and when any young animals are killed sometimes they offer up part of them as a sacrifice. These offerings when made by one of the heads of a family serve for the whole. I remember we often had them at my father's and my uncle's, and their families have been present. Some of our offerings are eaten with bitter herbs. We had a saying among us to anyone of a cross temper, 'That if they were to be eaten, they should be eaten with bitter herbs.'

We practised circumcision like the Jews and made offerings and feasts on that occasion in the same manner as they did. Like them also, our children were named from some event, some circumstance, or fancied foreboding at the time of their birth. I was named *Olaudah*, which in our language signifies vicissitude or fortunate; also, one favoured, and having a loud voice and well spoken. I remember we never polluted the name of the object of our adoration; on the contrary it was always mentioned with the greatest reverence, and we were totally unacquainted with swearing and all those terms of abuse and reproach which find their way so readily and copiously into the languages of more civilized people. The only expressions of that kind I remember were 'May you rot', or 'may you swell', or 'may a beast take you'.

I have before remarked that the natives of this part of Africa are extremely cleanly. This necessary habit of decency was with us a part of religion, and therefore we had many purifications and washings; indeed almost as many and used on the same occasions, if my recollection does not fail me, as the Jews. Those that touched the dead at any time were obliged to wash and purify themselves before they could enter a dwelling-house. Every woman too, at certain times, was forbidden to come into a dwelling-house or touch any person or anything we ate. I was so fond of my mother I could not keep from her or avoid touching her at some of those periods, in consequence of which I was obliged to be kept out with her in a little house made for that purpose till offering was made, and then we were purified.

Though we had no places of public worship, we had priests and magicians or wise men. I do not remember whether they had different offices or whether they were united in the same persons, but they were held in great reverence by the people. They calculated our time and

foretold events, as their name imported, for we called them
Ah-affoe-way-cah, which signifies calculators or yearly
men, our year being called Ah-affoe. They wore their
beards, and when they died they were succeeded by their
sons. Most of their implements and things of value were
interred along with them. Pipes and tobacco were also
put into the grave with the corpse, which was always
perfumed and ornamented, and animals were offered in
sacrifice to them. None accompanied their funerals but
those of the same profession or tribe. These buried them
after sunset and always returned from the grave by a
different way from that which they went.

These magicians were also our doctors or physicians.
They practised bleeding by cupping, and were very successful in healing wounds and expelling poisons. They had
likewise some extraordinary method of discovering jeal-
ousy, theft, and poisoning, the success of which no doubt
they derived from their unbounded influence over the
credulity and superstition of the people. I do not remember what those methods were, except that as to poisoning:
I recollect an instance or two, which I hope it will not be
deemed impertinent here to insert as it may serve as a kind
of specimen of the rest and is still used by the negroes in
the West Indies. A virgin had been poisoned but it was
not known by whom: the doctors ordered the corpse to be
taken up by some persons, and carried to the grave. As
soon as the bearers had raised it on their shoulders they
seemed seized with some sudden impulse, and ran to and
fro unable to stop themselves. At last, after having passed
through a number of thorns and prickly bushes unhurt, the
corpse fell from them close to a house and defaced it in the
fall, and the owner being taken up, he immediately
confessed the poisoning.

The natives are extremely cautious about poison. When
they buy any eatable the seller kisses it all round before

the buyer to show him it is not poisoned, and the same is done when any meat or drink is presented, particularly to a stranger. We have serpents of different kinds, some of which are esteemed ominous when they appear in our houses, and these we never molest. I remember two of those ominous snakes, each of which was as thick as the calf of a man's leg and in colour resembling a dolphin in the water, crept at different times into my mother's night-house where I always lay with her, and coiled themselves into folds, and each time they crowed like a cock. I was desired by some of the wise men to touch these that I might be interested in the good omens, which I did, for they were quite harmless and would tamely suffer themselves to be handled; and then they were put into a large open earthen pan and set on one side of the highway. Some of our snakes, however, were poisonous: one of them crossed the road one day when I was standing on it and passed between my feet without offering to touch me, to the great surprise of many who saw it; and these incidents were accounted by the wise men, and likewise by my mother and the rest of the people, as remarkable omens in my favour.

CHAPTER TWO

Kidnapped

My father, besides many slaves, had a numerous family of which seven lived to grow up, including myself and a sister who was the only daughter. As I was the youngest of the sons I became, of course, the greatest favourite with my mother and was always with her; and she used to take particular pains to form my mind. I was trained up from my earliest years in the art of war, my daily exercise was shooting and throwing javelins, and my mother adorned me with emblems after the manner of our greatest warriors. In this way I grew up till I was turned the age of 11, when an end was put to my happiness in the following manner. Generally when the grown people in the neighbourhood were gone far in the fields to labour, the children assembled together in some of the neighbours' premises to play, and commonly some of us used to get up a tree to look out for any assailant or kidnapper that might come upon us, for they sometimes took those opportunities of our parents' absence to attack and carry off as many as they could seize. One day, as I was watching at the top of a tree in our yard, I saw one of those people come into the yard of our next neighbour but one to kidnap, there being many stout young people in it. Immediately on this I gave the alarm of the rogue and he was surrounded by the stoutest of them, who entangled him with cords so that he could not escape till some of the

grown people came and secured him. But alas! ere long
it was my fate to be thus attacked and to be carried off
when none of the grown people were nigh. One day, when
all our people were gone out to their works as usual and
only I and my dear sister were left to mind the house, two
men and a woman got over our walls, and in a moment
seized us both, and without giving us time to cry out or
make resistance they stopped our mouths and ran off
with us into the nearest wood. Here they tied our hands
and continued to carry us as far as they could till night
came on, when we reached a small house where the robbers
halted for refreshment and spent the night. We were then
unbound but were unable to take any food, and being
quite overpowered by fatigue and grief, our only relief
was some sleep, which allayed our misfortune for a short
time. The next morning we left the house and continued
travelling all the day. For a long time we had kept to the
woods, but at last we came into a road which I believed I
knew. I had now some hopes of being delivered, for we had
advanced but a little way before I discovered some people
at a distance, on which I began to cry out for their assistance:
but my cries had no other effect than to make them tie me
faster and stop my mouth, and then they put me into a large
sack. They also stopped my sister's mouth and tied her
hands, and in this manner we proceeded till we were out of
the sight of these people. When we went to rest the following
night they offered us some victuals, but we refused it, and
the only comfort we had was in being in one another's
arms all that night and bathing each other with our tears.
But alas! we were soon deprived of even the small comfort
of weeping together. The next day proved a day of greater
sorrow than I had yet experienced, for my sister and I were
then separated while we lay clasped in each other's arms.
It was in vain that we besought them not to part us; she
was torn from me and immediately carried away, while

I was left in a state of distraction not to be described. I cried and grieved continually, and for several days I did not eat anything but what they forced into my mouth. At length, after many days' travelling, during which I had often changed masters, I got into the hands of a chieftain in a very pleasant country. This man had two wives and some children, and they all used me extremely well and did all they could to comfort me, particularly the first wife, who was something like my mother. Although I was a great many days' journey from my father's house, yet these people spoke exactly the same language with us. This first master of mine, as I may call him, was a smith, and my principal employment was working his bellows, which were the same kind as I had seen in my vicinity. They were in some respects not unlike the stoves here in gentlemen's kitchens, and were covered over with leather; and in the middle of that leather a stick was fixed, and a person stood up and worked it in the same manner as is done to pump water out of a cask with a hand pump. I believe it was gold he worked, for it was of a lovely bright yellow colour and was worn by the women on their wrists and ankles. I was there I suppose about a month, and they at last used to trust me some little distance from the house. This liberty I used in embracing every opportunity to inquire the way to my own home: and I also sometimes, for the same purpose, went with the maidens in the cool of the evenings to bring pitchers of water from the springs for the use of the house. I had also remarked where the sun rose in the morning and set in the evening as I had travelled along, and I had observed that my father's house was towards the rising of the sun. I therefore determined to seize the first opportunity of making my escape and to shape my course for that quarter, for I was quite oppressed and weighed down by grief after my mother and friends, and my love of liberty, ever great, was strengthened by the mortifying circumstance of not daring to eat with the free-born children, although I was mostly their companion. While I was projecting my escape, one day an unlucky event happened which quite disconcerted my plan and put an end to my hopes. I used to be sometimes employed in assisting an elderly woman slave to cook and take care of the poultry, and one morning, while I was feeding some chickens, I happened to toss a small pebble at one of them, which hit it on the middle and directly killed it. The old slave, having soon after missed the chicken, inquired after it; and on my relating the accident (for I told her the truth, because my mother would never suffer me to tell a lie) she flew into a violent passion, threatened that I should suffer for it, and, my master being out, she immediately went and told her mistress what I had done. This alarmed me very much and I expected an instant flogging, which to me was uncommonly dreadful, for I had seldom been beaten at home. I therefore resolved to fly, and accordingly I ran into a thicket that was hard by and hid myself in the bushes. Soon afterwards my mistress and the slave returned, and not seeing me they searched all the house, but not finding me, and I not making answer when they called to me, they thought I had run away and the whole neighbour-hood was raised in the pursuit of me. In that part of the country (as in ours) the houses and villages were skirted with woods or shrubberies, and the bushes were so thick that a man could readily conceal himself in them so as to elude the strictest search. The neighbours continued the whole day looking for me and several times many of them came within a few yards of the place where I lay hid. I then gave myself up for lost entirely, and expected every moment, when I heard a rustling among the trees, to be found out and punished by my master: but they never discovered me, though they were often so near that I even heard their conjectures as they were looking about for me;

and I now learned from them that any attempts to return home would be hopeless. Most of them supposed I had fled towards home, but the distance was so great and the way so intricate that they thought I could never reach it, and that I should be lost in the woods. When I heard this I was seized with a violent panic and abandoned myself to despair. Night too began to approach and aggravated all my fears. I had before entertained hopes of getting home and I had determined when it should be dark to make the attempt, but I was now convinced it was fruitless and began to consider that, if possibly I could escape all other animals, I could not those of the human kind; and that, not knowing the way, I must perish in the woods. Thus was I like the hunted deer:

'Ev'ry leaf and ev'ry whisp'ring breath
Convey'd a foe, and ev'ry foe a death.'

I heard frequent rustlings among the leaves, and being pretty sure they were snakes I expected every instant to be stung by them. This increased my anguish and the horror of my situation became now quite insupportable. I at length quitted the thicket, very faint and hungry for I had not eaten or drank anything all the day, and crept to my master's kitchen from whence I set out at first, and which was an open shed, and laid myself down in the ashes with an anxious wish for death to relieve me from all my pains. I was scarcely awake in the morning when the old woman slave, who was the first up, came to light the fire and saw me in the fireplace. She was very much surprised to see me and could scarcely believe her own eyes. She now promised to intercede for me and went for her master, who soon after came, and, having slightly reprimanded me, ordered me to be taken care of and not ill-treated.

Soon after this my master's only daughter and child

by his first wife sickened and died, which affected him so much that for some time he was almost frantic, and really would have killed himself had he not been watched and prevented. However, in a small time afterwards he recovered and I was again sold. I was now carried to the left of the sun's rising, through many different countries and a number of large woods. The people I was sold to used to carry me very often when I was tired either on their shoulders or on their backs. I saw many convenient well-built sheds along the roads at proper distances, to accommodate the merchants and travellers who lay in those buildings along with their wives, who often accompany them; and they always go well armed.

From the time I left my own nation I always found somebody that understood me till I came to the sea coast. The languages of different nations did not totally differ, nor were they so copious as those of the Europeans, particularly the English. They were therefore easily learned, and while I was journeying thus through Africa I acquired two or three different tongues. In this manner I had been travelling for a considerable time, when one evening, to my great surprise, whom should I see brought to the house where I was but my dear sister! As soon as she saw me she gave a loud shriek and ran into my arms – I was quite overpowered: neither of us could speak, but for a considerable time clung to each other in mutual embraces, unable to do anything but weep. Our meeting affected all who saw us, and indeed I must acknowledge, in honour of those sable destroyers of human rights, that I never met with any ill treatment or saw any offered to their slaves except tying them, when necessary, to keep them from running away. When these people knew we were brother and sister they indulged us to be together, and the man to whom I supposed we belonged lay with us, he in the middle while she and I held one another by the hands across his breast all night; and thus for a while we forgot our misfortunes in the joy of being together: but even this small comfort was soon to have an end, for scarcely had the fatal morning appeared when she was again torn from me for ever! I was now more miserable, if possible, than before. The small relief which her presence gave me from pain was gone, and the wretchedness of my situation was redoubled by my anxiety after her fate and my apprehensions lest her sufferings should be greater than mine, when I could not be with her to alleviate them. Yes, thou dear partner of all my childish sports! thou sharer of my joys and sorrows! happy should I have ever esteemed myself to encounter every misery for you, and to procure your freedom by the sacrifice of my own. Though you were early forced from my arms, your image has been always riveted in my heart, from which neither *time nor fortune* have been able to remove it; so that, while the thoughts of your sufferings have damped my prosperity, they have mingled with adversity and increased its bitterness. To that Heaven which protects the weak from the strong I commit the care of your innocence and virtues, if they have not already received their full reward and if your youth and delicacy have not long since fallen victims to the violence of the African trader, the pestilential stench of a Guinea ship, the seasoning in the European colonies, or the lash and lust of a brutal and unrelenting overseer.

I did not long remain after my sister. I was again sold and carried through a number of places till, after travelling a considerable time, I came to a town called Tinmah in the most beautiful country I had yet seen in Africa. It was extremely rich, and there were many rivulets which flowed through it and supplied a large pond in the centre of the town, where the people washed. Here I first saw and tasted coconuts, which I thought superior to any nuts I had ever tasted before; and the trees, which were loaded, were also interspersed amongst the houses, which had commodious shades adjoining and were in the same manner are ours, the insides being neatly plastered and whitewashed. Here I also saw and tasted for the first time sugar-cane. Their money consisted of little white shells the size of the finger-nail. I was sold here for 172 of them by a merchant who lived and brought me there. I had been about two or three days at his house when a wealthy widow, a neighbour of his, came there one evening, and brought with her an only son, a young gentleman about my own age and size. Here they saw me; and, having taken a fancy to me, I was bought of the merchant, and went home with them. Her house and premises were situated close to one of those rivulets I have mentioned, and were the finest I ever saw in Africa: they were very extensive, and she had a number of slaves to attend her. The next day I was washed and perfumed, and when meal-time came I was led into the presence of my mistress, and ate and drank before her with her son. This filled me with astonishment; and I could scarce help expressing my surprise that the young gentleman should suffer me, who was bound, to eat with him who was free; and not only so, but that he would not at any time either eat or drink till I had taken first, because I was the eldest, which was agreeable to our custom. Indeed everything here, and all their treatment of me, made me forget that I was a slave. The language of these people resembled ours so nearly that we understood each other perfectly. They had also the very same customs as we. There were likewise slaves daily to attend us, while my young master and I with other boys sported with our darts and bows and arrows, as I had been used to do at home. In this resemblance to my former happy state I passed about two months; and I now began to think I was to be adopted into the family, and was beginning to be reconciled to my situation, and to forget by degrees my misfortunes, when all at once the delusion vanished; for without the least previous knowledge, one morning early, while my dear master and companion was still asleep, I was wakened out of my reverie to fresh sorrow, and hurried away even amongst the uncircumcised.

Thus at the very moment I dreamed of the greatest happiness, I found myself most miserable; and it seemed as if fortune wished to give me this taste of joy only to render the reverse more poignant. The change I now experienced was as painful as it was sudden and unexpected. It was a change indeed from a state of bliss to a scene which is inexpressible by me, as it discovered to me an element I had never before beheld and till then had no idea of, and wherein such instances of hardship and cruelty continually occurred as I can never reflect on but with horror.

All the nations and people I had hitherto passed through resembled our own in their manner, customs, and language: but I came at length to a country the inhabitants of which differed from us in all those particulars. I was very much struck with this difference, especially when I came among a people who did not circumcise and ate without washing their hands. They cooked also in iron pots and had European cutlasses and crossbows, which were unknown to us, and fought with their fists amongst themselves. Their women were not so modest as ours, for they ate and drank and slept with their men. But above all, I was amazed to see no sacrifices or offerings among them. In some of those places the people ornamented themselves with scars, and likewise filed their teeth very sharp. They wanted sometimes to ornament me in the same manner, but I would not suffer them, hoping that I might some time be among a people who did not thus disfigure themselves, as I thought they did. At last I came to the banks of a large river, which was covered with canoes in which the people appeared to live with their household utensils and provisions of all kinds. I was beyond measure astonished at this, as I had never before seen any water larger than a pond or a rivulet: and my surprise was mingled with no small fear when I was put into one of these canoes and we began to paddle and move along the river. We continued going on thus till night, and when we came to land and made fires on the banks, each family by themselves, some dragged their canoes on shore, others stayed and cooked in theirs and laid in them all night. Those on the land had mats of which they made tents, some in the shape of little houses: in these we slept, and after the morning meal we embarked again and proceeded as before. I was often very much astonished to see some of the women, as well as the men, jump into the water, dive to the bottom, come up again, and swim about. Thus I continued to travel, sometimes by land, sometimes by water, through different countries and various nations, till at the end of six or seven months after I had been kidnapped I arrived at the sea coast.

CHAPTER THREE

The Slave Ship

THE first object which saluted my eyes when I arrived on the coast was the sea, and a slave ship which was then riding at anchor and waiting for its cargo. These filled me with astonishment, which was soon converted into terror when I was carried on board. I was immediately handled and tossed up to see if I were sound by some of the crew, and I was now persuaded that I had gotten into a world of bad spirits and that they were going to kill me. Their complexions too differing so much from ours, their long hair and the language they spoke (which was very different from any I had ever heard) united to confirm me in this belief. Indeed such were the horrors of my views and fears at the moment that, if ten thousand worlds had been my own, I would have freely parted with them all to have exchanged my condition with that of the meanest slave in my own country. When I looked round the ship too and saw a large furnace or copper boiling and a multitude of black people of every description chained together, every one of their countenances expressing dejection and sorrow, I no longer doubted of my fate; and quite overpowered with horror and anguish, I fell motionless on the deck and fainted. When I recovered a little I found some black people about me, who I believed were some of those who had brought me on board and had been receiving their pay; they talked to me in order to cheer me, but all in vain.

I asked them if we were not to be eaten by those white men with horrible looks, red faces, and loose hair. They told me I was not, and one of the crew brought me a small portion of spirituous liquor in a wine glass, but being afraid of him I would not take it out of his hand. One of the blacks therefore took it from him and gave it to me, and I took a little down my palate, which instead of reviving me, as they thought it would, threw me into the greatest consternation at the strange feeling it produced, having never tasted such any liquor before. Soon after this the blacks who brought me on board went off, and left me abandoned to despair.

I now saw myself deprived of all chance of returning to my native country or even the least glimpse of hope of gaining the shore, which I now considered as friendly; and I even wished for my former slavery in preference to my present situation, which was filled with horrors of every kind, still heightened by my ignorance of what I was to undergo. I was not long suffered to indulge my grief; I was soon put down under the decks, and there I received such a salutation in my nostrils as I had never experienced in my life: so that with the loathsomeness of the stench and crying together, I became so sick and low that I was not able to eat, nor had I the least desire to taste anything. I now wished for the last friend, death, to relieve me; but soon, to my grief, two of the white men offered me eatables, and on my refusing to eat, one of them held me fast by the hands and laid me across I think the windlass, and tied my feet while the other flogged me severely. I had never experienced anything of this kind before, and although, not being used to the water, I naturally feared that element the first time I saw it, yet nevertheless could I have got over the nettings I would have jumped over the side, but I could not; and besides, the crew used to watch us very closely who were not chained down to the decks, lest we should leap into the water: and I have seen some of these poor African prisoners most severely cut for attempting to do so, and hourly whipped for not eating. This indeed was often the case with myself. In a little time after, amongst the poor chained men I found some of my own nation, which in a small degree gave ease to my mind. I inquired of these what was to be done with us; they gave me to understand we were to be carried to these white people's country to work for them. I then was a little revived, and thought if it were no worse than working, my situation was not so desperate: but still I feared I should be put to death, the white people looked and acted, as I thought, in so savage a manner; for I had never seen among my people such instances of brutal cruelty, and this not only shewn towards us blacks but also to some of the whites themselves. One white man in particular I saw, when we were permitted to be on deck, flogged so unmercifully with a large rope near the foremast that he died in consequence of it; and they tossed him over the side as they would have done a brute. This made me fear these people the more, and I expected nothing less than to be treated in the same manner. I could not help expressing my fears and apprehensions to some of my countrymen: I asked them if these people had no country but lived in this hollow place (the ship): they told me they did not, but came from a distant one. 'Then,' said I, 'how comes it in all our country we never heard of them?' They told me because they lived so very far off. I then asked where were their women? had they any like themselves? I was told they had: 'and why,' said I, 'do we not see them?' They answered, because they were left behind. I asked how the vessel could go? They told me they could not tell, but that there were cloths put upon the masts by the help of the ropes I saw, and then the vessel went on; and the white men had some spell or magic they put in the water when they liked in order to stop the vessel. I was exceedingly amazed at this account and really thought they were spirits. I therefore wished much to be from amongst them for I expected they would sacrifice me: but my wishes were vain, for we were so quartered that it was impossible for any of us to make our escape. While we stayed on the coast I was mostly on deck, and one day, to my great astonishment, I saw one of these vessels coming in with the sails up. As soon as the whites saw it they gave a great shout, at which we were amazed; and the more so as the vessel appeared larger by approaching nearer. At last she came to an anchor in my sight, and when the anchor was let go I and my countrymen who saw it were lost in astonishment to observe the vessel stop, and were now convinced it was done by magic. Soon after this the other ship got her boats out, and they came on board of us, and the people of both ships seemed very glad to see each other. Several of the strangers also shook hands with us black people, and made motions with their hands, signifying I suppose we were to go to their country; but we did not understand them. At last, when the ship we were in had got in all her cargo, they made ready with many fearful noises, and we were all put under deck so that we could not see how they managed the vessel. But this disappointment was the last of my sorrow. The stench of the hold while we were on the coast was so intolerably loathsome that it was dangerous to remain there for any time, and some of us had been permitted to stay on the deck for the fresh air; but now that the whole ship's cargo were confined together it became absolutely pestilential. The closeness of the place and the heat of the climate, added to the number in the ship, which was so crowded that each had scarcely room to turn himself, almost suffocated us. This produced copious perspirations, so that the air soon became unfit for respiration from a variety of loathsome smells, and brought on a sickness among the slaves, of which many died, thus falling victims to the improvident avarice, as I may call it, of their purchasers. This wretched situation was again aggravated by the galling of the chains, now become insupportable, and the filth of the necessary tubs, into which the children often fell and were almost suffocated. The shrieks of the women and the groans of the dying rendered the whole a scene of horror almost inconceivable. Happily perhaps for myself I was soon reduced so low here that it was thought necessary to keep me almost always on deck, and from my extreme youth I was not put in fetters. In this situation I expected every hour to share the fate of my companions, some of whom were almost daily brought upon deck at the point of death, which I began to hope would soon put an end to my miseries. Often did I think many of the inhabitants of the deep much more happy than myself. I envied them the freedom they enjoyed, and as often wished I could change my condition for theirs. Every circumstance I met with served only to render my state more painful, and heighten my apprehensions and my opinion of the cruelty of the whites. One day they had taken a number of fishes, and when they had killed and satisfied themselves with as many as they thought fit, to our astonishment who were on the deck, rather than give any of them to us to eat as we expected, they tossed the remaining fish into the sea again, although we begged and prayed for some as well as we could, but in vain; and some of my countrymen, being pressed by hunger, took an opportunity when they thought no one saw them of trying to get a little privately; but they were discovered, and the attempt procured them some very severe floggings. One day, when we had a smooth sea and moderate wind, two of my wearied countrymen who were chained together (I was near them at the time), preferring death to such a life of misery, somehow made through the nettings and jumped into the sea:

immediately another quite dejected fellow, who on account of his illness was suffered to be out of irons, also followed their example; and I believe many more would very soon have done the same if they had not been prevented by the ship's crew, who were instantly alarmed. Those of us that were the most active were in a moment put down under the deck, and there was such a noise and confusion amongst the people of the ship as I never heard before, to stop her and get the boat out to go after the slaves. However two of the wretches were drowned, but they got the other and afterwards flogged him unmercifully for thus attempting to prefer death to slavery. In this manner we continued to undergo more hardships than I can now relate, hardships which are inseparable from this accursed trade. Many a time we were near suffocation from the want of fresh air, which we were often without for whole days together. This and the stench of the necessary tubs carried off many. During our passage I first saw flying fishes, which surprised me very much: they used frequently to fly across the ship and many of them fell on the deck. I also now first saw the use of the quadrant; I had often with astonishment seen the mariners make observations with it, and I could not think what it meant. They at last took notice of my surprise, and one of them, willing to increase it as well as to gratify my curiosity, made me one day look through it. The clouds appeared to me to be land, which disappeared as they passed along. This heightened my wonder, and I was now more persuaded than ever that I was in another world and that everything about me was magic. At last we came in sight of the island of Barbados, at which the whites on board gave a great shout and made many signs of joy to us. We did not know what to think of this, but as the vessel drew nearer we plainly saw the harbour and other ships of different kinds and sizes, and we soon anchored amongst them off Bridgetown. Many merchants and

planters now came on board, though it was in the evening.
They put us in separate parcels and examined us attentively.
They also made us jump, and pointed to the land, signifying
we were to go there. We thought by this we should be
eaten by these ugly men, as they appeared to us; and
when soon after we were all put down under the deck
again, there was much dread and trembling among us,
and nothing but bitter cries to be heard all the night from
these apprehensions, insomuch that at last the white people
got some old slaves from the land to pacify us. They told
us we were not to be eaten but to work, and were soon to
go on land where we should see many of our country people.
This report eased us much; and sure enough soon after
we were landed there came to us Africans of all languages.
We were conducted immediately to the merchant's yard,
where we were all pent up together like so many sheep in
a fold without regard to sex or age. As every object was
new to me everything I saw filled me with surprise. What
struck me first was that the houses were built with storeys,
and in every other respect different from those in Africa:
but I was still more astonished on seeing people on horseback. I did not know what this could mean, and indeed I
thought these people were full of nothing but magical arts.
While I was in this astonishment one of my fellow prisoners
spoke to a countryman of his about the horses, who said
they were the same kind they had in their country. I
understood them though they were from a distant part of
Africa, and I thought it odd I had not seen any horses
there; but afterwards when I came to converse with
different Africans I found they had many horses amongst
them, and much larger than those I then saw. We were
not many days in the merchant's custody before we were
sold after their usual manner, which is this: On a signal
given, (as the beat of a drum) the buyers rush at once into
the yard where the slaves are confined, and make choice

of that parcel they like best. The noise and clamour with which this is attended and the eagerness visible in the countenances of the buyers serve not a little to increase the apprehensions of the terrified Africans, who may well be supposed to consider them as the ministers of that destruction to which they think themselves devoted. In this manner, without scruple, are relations and friends separated, most of them never to see each other again. I remember in the vessel in which I was brought over, in the men's apartment there were several brothers who, in the sale, were sold in different lots; and it was very moving on this occasion to see and hear their cries at parting. O, ye nominal Christians! might not an African ask you, Learned you this from your God who says unto you, Do unto all men as you would men should do unto you? Is it not enough that we are torn from our country and friends to toil for your luxury and lust of gain? Must every tender feeling be likewise sacrificed to your avarice? Are the dearest friends and relations, now rendered more dear by their separation from their kindred, still to be parted from each other and thus prevented from cheering the gloom of slavery with the small comfort of being together and mingling their sufferings and sorrows? Why are parents to lose their children, brothers their sisters, or husbands their wives? Surely this is a new refinement in cruelty which, while it has no advantage to atone for it, thus aggravates distress and adds fresh horrors even to the wretchedness of slavery.

CHAPTER FOUR

Voyage to England

I now totally lost the small remains of comfort I had enjoyed in conversing with my countrymen; the women too who used to wash and take care of me were all gone different ways, and I never saw one of them afterwards.

I stayed in this island for a few days, I believe it could not be above a fortnight, when I and some few more slaves that were not saleable amongst the rest, from very much fretting, were shipped off in a sloop for North America. On the passage we were better treated than when we were coming from Africa and we had plenty of rice and fat pork. We were landed up a river a good way from the sea, about Virgina county, where we saw few or none of our native Africans and not one soul who could talk to me. I was a few weeks weeding grass and gathering stones in a plantation, and at last all my companions were distributed different ways and only myself was left. I was now exceedingly miserable and thought myself worse off than any of the rest of my companions, for they could talk to each other, but I had no person to speak to that I could understand. In this state I was constantly grieving and pining and wishing for death rather than anything else. While I was in this plantation the gentleman to whom I suppose the estate belonged being unwell, I was one day sent for to his dwelling house to fan him; when I came into the room where he was I was very much affrighted at some

things I saw, and the more so as I had seen a black woman
slave as I came through the house who was cooking the
dinner, and the poor creature was cruelly loaded with
various kinds of iron machines; she had one particularly
on her head which locked her mouth so fast that she could
scarcely speak, and could not eat nor drink. I was much
astonished and shocked at this contrivance, which I
afterwards learned was called the iron muzzle. Soon after
I had a fan put into my hand to fan the gentleman while he
slept, and so I did indeed with great fear. While he was
fast asleep I indulged myself a great deal in looking about
the room, which to me appeared very fine and curious.
The first object that engaged my attention was a watch
which hung on the chimney and was going. I was quite
surprised at the noise it made and was afraid it would
tell the gentleman anything I might do amiss: and when
I immediately after observed a picture hanging in the
room which appeared constantly to look at me, I was still
more affrighted, having never seen such things as these
before. At one time I thought it was something relative
to magic, and not seeing it move I thought it might be
some way the whites had to keep their great men when
they died and offer them libation as we used to do to our
friendly spirits. In this state of anxiety I remained till
my master awoke, when I was dismissed out of the room
to my no small satisfaction and relief, for I thought that
these people were all made up of wonders. In this place
I was called Jacob, but on board the *African* snow I was
called Michael. I had been some time in this miserable,
forlorn, and much dejected state without having anyone
to talk to, which made my life a burden, when the kind and
unknown hand of the Creator (who in very deed leads the
blind in a way they know not) now began to appear, to my
comfort; for one day the captain of a merchant ship called
the *Industrious Bee* came on some business to my master's

house. This gentleman, whose name was Michael Henry Pascal, was a lieutenant in the Royal Navy, but now commanded this trading ship which was somewhere in the confines of the county many miles off. While he was at my master's house it happened that he saw me and liked me so well that he made a purchase of me. I think I have often heard him say he gave thirty or forty pounds sterling for me, but I do not now remember which. However, he meant me for a present to some of his friends in England, and I was sent accordingly from the house of my then master, one Mr Campbell, to the place where the ship lay; I was conducted on horseback by an elderly black man, (a mode of travelling which appeared very odd to me). When I arrived I was carried on board a fine large ship, loaded with tobacco, etc. and just ready to sail for England. I now thought my condition much mended; I had sails to lie on and plenty of good victuals to eat, and everybody on board used me very kindly, quite contrary to what I had seen of any white people before; I therefore began to think that they were not all of the same disposition. A few days after I was on board we sailed for England. I was still at a loss to conjecture my destiny. By this time however I could smatter a little imperfect English, and I wanted to know as well as I could where we were going. Some of the people of the ship used to tell me they were going to carry me back to my own country and this made me very happy. I was quite rejoiced at the sound of going back, and thought if I should get home what wonders I should have to tell. But I was reserved for another fate and was soon undeceived when we came within sight of the English coast. While I was on board this ship, my captain and master named me *Gustavus Vasa*. I at that time began to understand him a little, and refused to be called so, and told him as well as I could that I would be called Jacob; but he said I should not, and still called me Gustavus; and when I refused to answer to my new name, which at first I did, it gained me many a cuff; so at length I submitted and was obliged to bear the present name, by which I have been known ever since. The ship had a very long passage, and on that account we had very short allowance of provisions. Towards the last we had only one pound and a half of bread per week, and about the same quantity of meat, and one quart of water a day. We spoke with only one vessel the whole time we were at sea, and but once we caught a few fishes. In our extremities the captain and people told me in jest they would kill and eat me, but I thought them in earnest and was depressed beyond measure, expecting every moment to be my last. While I was in this situation, one evening they caught, with a good deal of trouble, a large shark, and got it on board. This gladdened my poor heart exceedingly, as I thought it would serve the people to eat instead of their eating me; but very soon, to my astonishment, they cut off a small part of the tail and tossed the rest over the side. This renewed my consternation, and I did not know what to think of these white people, though I very much feared they would kill and eat me. There was on board the ship a young lad who had never been at sea before, about four or five years older than myself: his name was Richard Baker. He was a native of America, had received an excellent education, and was of a most amiable temper. Soon after I went on board he showed me a great deal of partiality and attention and in return I grew extremely fond of him. We at length became inseparable, and for the space of two years he was of very great use to me and was my constant companion and instructor. Although this dear youth had many slaves of his own, yet he and I have gone through many sufferings together on shipboard, and we have many nights lain in each other's bosoms when we were in great distress. Thus such a friendship was cemented between us as we cherished till his death, which to my very great sorrow happened in the year 1759, when he was up the Archipelago on board his Majesty's ship the *Preston*, an event which I have never ceased to regret as I lost at once a kind interpreter, an agreeable companion, and a faithful friend; who, at the age of fifteen, discovered a mind superior to prejudice, and who was not ashamed to notice, to associate with, and to be the friend and instructor of one who was ignorant, a stranger, of a different complexion, and a slave! My master had lodged in his mother's house in America: he respected him very much and made him always eat with him in the cabin. He used often to tell him jocularly that he would kill me to eat. Sometimes he would say to me the black people were not good to eat, and would ask me if we did not eat people in my country. I said, No: then he said he would kill Dick (as he always called him) first, and afterwards me. Though this hearing relieved my mind a little as to myself, I was alarmed for Dick and whenever he was called I used to be very much afraid he was to be killed, and I would peep and watch to see if they were going to kill him: nor was I free from this consternation till we made the land. One night we lost a man overboard, and the cries and noise were so great and confused in stopping the ship, that I, who did not know what was the matter, began as usual to be very much afraid and to think they were going to make an offering with me and perform some magic, which I still believed they dealt in. As the waves were very high I thought the Ruler of the seas was angry, and I expected to be offered up to appease him. This filled my mind with agony, and I could not any more that night close my eyes to rest. However when daylight appeared I was a little eased in my mind, but still every time I was called I used to think it was to be killed. Some time after this we saw some very large fish, which I afterwards found were called grampuses. They looked to me extremely terrible and made their appearance just at dusk, and were so near as to blow the water on the ship's deck. I believed them to be the rulers of the sea, and as the white people did not make any offerings at any time I thought they were angry with them: and at last, what confirmed my belief was, the wind just then died away and a calm ensued, and in consequence of it the ship stopped going. I supposed that the fish had performed this, and I hid myself in the fore part of the ship through fear of being offered up to appease them, every minute peeping and quaking: but my good friend Dick came shortly towards me, and I took an opportunity to ask him, as well as I could, what these fish were. Not being able to talk much English, I could but just make him understand my question, and not at all when I asked him if any offerings were to be made to them: however, he told me these fish would swallow anybody, which sufficiently alarmed me. Here he was called away by the captain, who was leaning over the quarter-deck railing and looking at the fish, and most of the people were busied in getting a barrel of pitch to light for them to play with. The captain now called me to him, having learned some of my apprehensions from Dick, and having diverted himself and others for some time with my fears, which appeared ludicrous enough in my crying and trembling, he dismissed me. The barrel of pitch was now lighted and put over the side into the water: by this time it was just dark, and the fish went after it, and to my great joy I saw them no more.

However, all my alarms began to subside when we got sight of land, and at last the ship arrived at Falmouth after a passage of thirteen weeks. Every heart on board seemed gladdened on our reaching the shore, and none more than mine. The captain immediately went on shore and sent on board some fresh provisions, which we wanted very much: we made good use of them and our famine was soon turned into feasting almost without ending. It was about the beginning of 1757 when I arrived in England, and I was near twelve years of age at that time. I was very much struck with the buildings and the pavement of the streets in Falmouth, and indeed any object I saw filled me with new surprise. One morning when I got upon deck, I saw it covered all over with the snow that fell overnight: as I had never seen anything of the kind before I thought it was salt, so I immediately ran down to the mate and desired him, as well as I could, to come and see how somebody in the night had thrown salt all over the deck. He, knowing what it was, desired me to bring some of it down to him: accordingly I took up a handful of it, which I found very cold indeed, and when I brought it to him he desired me to taste it. I did so, and I was surprised beyond measure. I then asked him what it was; he told me it was snow, but I could not in anywise understand him. He asked me if we had no such thing in my country, and I told him, No. I then asked him the use of it and who made it; he told me a great man in the heavens, called God: but here again I was to all intents and purposes at a loss to understand him, and the more so when a little after I saw the air filled with it in a heavy shower which fell down on the same day. After this I went to church, and having never been at such a place before I was again amazed at seeing and hearing the service. I asked all I could about it, and they gave me to understand it was worshipping God, who made us and all things. I was still at a great loss, and soon got into an endless field of inquiries, as well as I was able to speak and ask about things. However, my little friend Dick used to be my best interpreter, for I could make free with him and he always instructed me with pleasure: and from what I could understand by him of this God, and in seeing these white people did not sell one another as we did, I was much pleased; and in this I thought they were much happier than we Africans. I was astonished at the wisdom of the white people in all things I saw, but was amazed at their not sacrificing or making any offerings, and eating with unwashed hands and touching the dead. I likewise could not help remarking the particular slenderness of their women, which I did not at first like, and I thought they were not so modest and shamefaced as the African women.

I had often seen my master and Dick employed in reading, and I had a great curiosity to talk to the books as I thought they did, and so to learn how all things had a beginning: for that purpose I have often taken up a book and have talked to it and then put my ears to it, when alone, in hopes it would answer me; and I have been very much concerned when I found it remained silent.

My master lodged at the house of a gentleman in Falmouth who had a fine little daughter about six or seven years of age, and she grew prodigiously fond of me, insomuch that we used to eat together and had servants to wait on us. I was so much caressed by this family that it often reminded me of the treatment I had received from my little noble African master. After I had been here a few days I was sent on board of the ship, but the child cried so much after me that nothing could pacify her till I was sent for again. It is ludicrous enough, that I began to fear I should be betrothed to this young lady, and when my master asked me if I would stay there with her behind him, as he was going away with the ship which had taken in the tobacco again, I cried immediately and said I would not leave him. At last by stealth one night I was sent on board the ship again, and in a little time we sailed for Guernsey where she was in part owned by a merchant, one Nicholas Doberry. As I was now amongst a people who had not their faces scarred like some of the African nations where I had been. I was very glad I did not let them ornament me in that manner when I was with them. When we arrived at Guernsey, my master placed me to board and lodge with one of his mates who had a wife and family there; and some months afterwards he went to England and left me in care of this mate, together with my friend Dick. This mate had a little daughter, aged about five or six years, with whom I used to be much delighted. I had often observed that when her mother washed her face it looked very rosy, but when she washed mine it did not look so: I therefore tried often times myself if I could not by washing make my face of the same colour as my little playmate (Mary), but it was all in vain, and I now began to be mortified at the difference in our complexions. This woman behaved to me with great kindness and attention, and taught me every-thing in the same manner as she did her own child, and indeed in every respect treated me as such. I remained here till the summer of the year 1757, when my master, being appointed first lieutenant of His Majesty's ship the *Roebuck* sent for Dick and me and his old mate: on this we all left Guernsey and set out for England in a sloop bound for London. As we were coming up towards the Nore where the *Roebuck* lay, a man-of-war's boat came alongside to press our people, on which each man ran to hide himself. I was very much frightened at this, though I did not know what it meant or what to think or do. However, I went and hid myself also under a hencoop. Immediately afterwards the press-gang came on board with their swords drawn, and searched all about, pulled the people out by force, and put them into the boat. At last I was found out also: the man that found me held me up by the heels while they all made their sport of me, I roaring and crying out all the time most lustily: but at last the mate, who was my con-ductor, seeing this, came to my assistance and did all he could to pacify me, but all to very little purpose till I had seen the boat go off. Soon afterwards we came to the Nore where the *Roebuck* lay, and to our great joy my master came on board to us and brought us to the ship. When I went on board this large ship I was amazed indeed to see the quantity of men and guns. However my surprise began to diminish as my knowledge increased, and I ceased to feel those apprehensions and alarms which had taken such strong possession of me when I first came among the Europeans, and for some time after. I began now to pass to an opposite extreme; I was so far from being afraid of anything new which I saw that, after I had been some time in this ship, I even began to long for a battle. My griefs too, which in young minds are not perpetual, were now wearing away, and I soon enjoyed myself pretty well and felt tolerably easy in my present situation.

CHAPTER FIVE

War at Sea

I T was now between two and three years since I first came
to England, a great part of which I had spent at sea; so
that I became inured to that service and began to consider
myself happily situated, for my master treated me always
extremely well, and my attachment and gratitude to him
were very great. From the various scenes I had beheld on
shipboard I soon grew a stranger to terror of every kind and
was, in that respect at least, almost an Englishman. I have
often reflected with surprise that I never felt half the alarm
at any of the numerous dangers I have been in that I was
filled with at the first sight of the Europeans and at every
act of theirs, even the most trifling, when I first came
among them and for some time afterwards. That fear,
however, which was the effect of my ignorance, wore
away as I began to know them. I could now speak English
tolerably well and I perfectly understood everything that
was said. I now not only felt myself quite easy with these
new countrymen but relished their society and manners. I
no longer looked upon them as spirits, but as men superior
to us, and therefore I had the stronger desire to resemble
them, to imbibe their spirit and imitate their manners; I
therefore embraced every occasion of improvement, and
every new thing that I observed I treasured up in my
memory. I had long wished to be able to read and write, and
for this purpose I took every opportunity to gain instruction,

but had made as yet very little progress. However, when I went to London with my master I had soon an opportunity of improving myself, which I gladly embraced. Shortly after my arrival he sent me to wait upon the Miss Guerins, who had treated me with much kindness when I was there before; and they sent me to school.

While I was attending these ladies their servants told me I could not go to Heaven unless I was baptized. This made me very uneasy, for I had now some faint idea of a future state: accordingly I communicated my anxiety to the eldest Miss Guerin, with whom I was become a favourite, and pressed her to have me baptized; when to my great joy, she told me I should. She had formerly asked my master to let me be baptized but he had refused; however she now insisted on it, and he being under some obligation to her brother complied with her request, so I was baptized in St Margaret's Church, Westminster, in Feburary 1759, by my present name. The clergyman at the same time gave me a book called a Guide to the Indians, written by the Bishop of Sodor and Man. On this occasion Miss Guerin did me the honour to stand as godmother and afterward gave me a treat. I used to attend these ladies about the town, in which service I was extremely happy, as I had thus many opportunities of seeing London which I desired of all things. I was sometimes however with my master at his rendezvous-house, which was at the foot of Westminster Bridge. Here I used to enjoy myself in playing about the bridge stairs and often in the watermen's wherries, with other boys. On one of these occasions there was another boy with me in a wherry, and we went out into the current of the river: while we were there two more stout boys came to us in another wherry, and abusing us for taking the boat, desired me to get into the other wherry-boat. Accordingly I went to get out of the wherry I was in, but just as I had got one of my feet into the other boat the boys shoved it off, so that I fell into the Thames, and not being able to swim, I should unavoidably have been drowned but for the assistance of some watermen who providentially came to my relief.

The *Namur* being again got ready for sea, my master with his gang was ordered on board, and to my no small grief I was obliged to leave my schoolmaster, whom I liked very much and always attended while I stayed in London, to repair on board with my master. Nor did I leave my kind patronesses, the Miss Guerins, without uneasiness and regret. They often used to teach me to read and took great pains to instruct me in the principles of religion and the knowledge of God. I therefore parted from those amiable ladies with reluctance, after receiving from them many friendly cautions how to conduct myself and some valuable presents.

When I came to Spithead, I found we were destined for the Mediterranean with a large fleet which was now ready to put to sea. We only waited for the arrival of the Admiral who soon came on board, and about the beginning of the spring 1759, having weighed anchor and got under way, sailed for the Mediterranean; and in eleven days from the Land's End we got to Gibralter. While we were here I used to be often on shore and got various fruits in great plenty and very cheap.

I had frequently told several people in my excursions on shore the story of my being kidnapped with my sister, and of our being separated as I have related before; and I had as often expressed my anxiety for her fate and my sorrow at having never met her again. One day when I was on shore, and mentioning these circumstances to some persons, one of them told me he knew where my sister was, and if I would accompany him he would bring me to her. Improbable as this story was I believed it immediately and agreed to go with him, while my heart leaped for joy: and indeed he conducted me to a black young woman who was so like my sister that, at first sight, I really thought it was her: but I was quickly undeceived, and on talking to her I found her to be of another nation.

While we lay here the *Preston* came in from the Levant. As soon as she arrived, my master told me I should now see my old companion, Dick, who had gone in her when she sailed for Turkey. I was much rejoiced at this news and expected every minute to embrace him, and when the captain came on board of our ship, which he did immediately after, I ran to inquire after my friend; but with inexpressible sorrow I learned from the boat's crew that the dear youth was dead! and that they had brought his chest and all his other things to my master: these he afterwards gave to me and I regarded them as a memorial of my friend, whom I loved and grieved for as a brother.

Here we remained with all our sails unbent, while the fleet was watering and doing other necessary things. While we were in this situation, one day the Admiral, with most of the principal officers and many people of all stations being on shore, about seven o'clock in the evening we were alarmed by signals from the frigates stationed for that purpose, and in an instant there was a general cry that the French fleet was out, and just passing through the Straits. The Admiral immediately came on board with some other officers, and it is impossible to describe the noise, hurry and confusion throughout the fleet, in bending their sails and shipping their cables; many people and ships' boats were left on shore in the bustle. We had two captains on board of our ship who came away in the hurry and left their ships to follow. We showed lights from the gunwale to the main topmast-head; and all our lieutenants were employed amongst the fleet to tell the ships not to wait for their captains, but to put the sails to the yards, slip their cables and follow us; and in this confusion of making

ready for fighting we set out for sea in the dark after the
French fleet. Here I could have exclaimed with Ajax,

> 'O Jove! O father! if it be thy will
> That we must perish, we thy will obey,
> But let us perish by the light of day.'

They had got the start of us so far that we were not able to
come up with them during the night, but at daylight we
saw seven sail of the line of battle some miles ahead. We
immediately chased them till about four o'clock in the
evening, when our ships came up with them, and though
we were about fifteen large ships, our gallant Admiral only
fought them with his own division, which consisted of seven,
so that we were just ship to ship. We passed by the whole
of the enemy's fleet in order to come at their Commander,
Mons. La Clue, who was in the *Ocean*, an eighty-four-gun
ship: as we passed they all fired on us, and at one time
three of them fired together, continuing to do so for some
time. Notwithstanding which our Admiral would not suffer
a gun to be fired at any of them, to my astonishment, but
made us lie on our bellies on the deck till we came quite
close to the *Ocean*, who was ahead of them all, when we had
orders to pour the whole three tiers into her at once.

The engagement now commenced with great fury on
both sides: the *Ocean* immediately returned our fire and we
continued engaged with each other for some time, during
which I was frequently stunned with the thundering of the
great guns, whose dreadful contents hurried many of my
companions into awful eternity. At last the French line was
entirely broken and we obtained the victory, which was
immediately proclaimed with loud huzzas and acclamations. We took three prizes, *La Modeste*, of sixty-four guns,
and *Le Temeraire* and *Centaur*, of seventy-four guns each.
The rest of the French ships took to flight with all the sail

they could crowd. Our ships being very much damaged and quite disabled from pursuing the enemy, the Admiral immediately quitted her and went, in the broken and only boat we had left, on board the *Newark*, with which and some other ships he went after the French. The *Ocean* and another large French ship called the *Redoubtable*, endeavouring to escape, ran ashore at Cape Logas on the coast of Portugal, and the French Admiral and some of the crew got ashore; but we, finding it impossible to get the ships off, set fire to them both. About midnight I saw the *Ocean* blow up with a most dreadful explosion. I never beheld a more awful scene. In less than a minute the midnight for a certain space seemed turned into day by the blaze, which was attended with a noise louder and more terrible than thunder, that seemed to rend every element around us.

My station during the engagement was on the middle-deck, where I was quartered with another boy to bring powder to the aftermost gun, and here I was a witness of the dreadful fate of many of my companions who, in the twinkling of an eye, were dashed in pieces and launched into eternity. Happily I escaped unhurt though the shot and splinters flew thick about me during the whole fight. Towards the latter part of it my master was wounded and I saw him carried down to the surgeon, but though I was much alarmed for him and wished to assist him I dared not leave my post. At this station my gun-mate (a partner in bringing powder for the same gun) and I ran a very great risk for more than half an hour of blowing up the ship. For when we had taken the cartridges out of the boxes, the bottoms of many of them proving rotten, the powder ran all about the deck near the match tub: we scarcely had water enough at the last to throw on it. We were also, from our employment, very much exposed to the enemy's shots, for we had to go through nearly the whole length of the ship to bring the powder. I expected therefore every minute to be my last, especially when I saw our men fall so thick about me, but wishing to guard as much against the dangers as possible, at first I thought it would be safest not to go for the powder till the Frenchmen had fired their broadside, and then while they were charging I could go and come with my powder: but immediately afterwards I thought this caution was fruitless, and cheering myself with the reflection that there was a time allotted for me to die as well as to be born, I instantly cast off all fear or thought whatever of death and went through the whole of my duty with alacrity, pleasing myself with the hope, if I survived the battle, of relating it and the dangers I had escaped to the dear Miss Guerins and others, when I should return to London.

Our ship suffered very much in this engagement, for besides the number of our killed and wounded, she was almost torn to pieces and our rigging so much shattered that our mizen-mast and main-yard, etc. hung over the side of the ship; so that we were obliged to get many carpenters and others from some of the ships of the fleet to assist in setting us in some tolerable order, and notwithstanding, it took us some time before we were completely refitted; after which we left Admiral Broderick to command, and we, with the prizes, steered for England. On the passage and as soon as my master was something recovered of his wounds, the Admiral appointed him captain of the *Ætna* fire-ship, on which he and I left the *Namur* and went on board of her at sea. I liked this little ship very much. I now became the captain's steward, in which situation I was very happy, for I was extremely well treated by all on board, and I had leisure to improve myself in reading and writing. The latter I had learned a little of before I left the *Namur*, as there was a school on board. When we arrived at Spithead the *Ætna* went into Portsmouth harbour to refit, which being done, we returned

to Spithead and joined a large fleet that was thought to be
intended against the *Havannah*, but about that time the king
died: whether that prevented the expedition I know not,
but it caused our ship to be stationed at Cowes in the Isle of
Wight till the beginning of the year sixty-one. Here I spent
my time very pleasantly; I was much on shore all about this
delightful island, and found the inhabitants very civil.

While I was here, I met with a trifling incident, which
surprised me agreeably. I was one day in a field belonging
to a gentleman who had a black boy about my own size;
this boy having observed me from his master's house was
transported at the sight of one of his own countrymen, and
ran to meet me with the utmost haste. I not knowing what
he was about turned a little out of his way at first, but to no
purpose: he soon came close to me and caught hold of me
in his arms as if I had been his brother, though we had
never seen each other before. After we had talked together
for some time he took me to his master's house, where I was
treated very kindly. This benevolent boy and I were very
happy in frequently seeing each other till about the month
of March 1761, when our ship had orders to fit out again
for another expedition. When we got ready, we joined a
very large fleet at Spithead, commanded by Commodore
Keppel, which was destined against Belle-Isle, and with a
number of transport ships with troops on board to make a
descent on the place. We sailed once more in quest of fame.
I longed to engage in new adventures and see fresh wonders.

I had a mind on which everything uncommon made its
full impression, and every event which I considered as
marvellous. Every extraordinary escape or signal deliverance, either of myself or others, I looked upon to be effected
by the interposition of Providence. We had not been above
ten days at sea before an incident of this kind happened
which, whatever credit it may obtain from the reader,
made no small impression on my mind.

We had on board a gunner, whose name was John Mondle, a man of very indifferent morals. This man's cabin was between the decks, exactly over where I lay, abreast of the quarter-deck ladder. One night, 20 April, being terrified with a dream, he awoke in so great a fright that he could not rest in his bed any longer nor even remain in his cabin, and he went upon deck about four o'clock in the morning extremely agitated. He immediately told those on the deck of the agonies of his mind and the dream which occasioned it, in which he said he had seen many things very awful and had been warned by St Peter to repent, who told him time was short. This he said had greatly alarmed him and he was determined to alter his life. People generally mock the fears of others when they are themselves in safety, and some of his shipmates who heard him only laughed at him. However he made a vow that he never would drink strong liquors again, and he immediately got a light and gave away his sea-stores of liquor. After which, his agitation still continuing, he began to read the Scriptures, hoping to find some relief, and soon afterwards he laid himself down again on his bed and endeavoured to compose himself to sleep, but to no purpose, his mind still continuing in a state of agony. By this time it was exactly half after seven in the morning: I was then under the half-deck at the great cabin door, and all at once I heard the people in the waist cry out most fearfully – 'The Lord have mercy upon us! We are all lost! The Lord have mercy upon us!' Mr Mondle hearing the cries immediately ran out of his cabin, and we were instantly struck by the *Lynne*, a forty-gun ship, Captain Clark, which nearly ran us down. This ship had just put about and was by the wind, but had not got full headway or we must all have perished, for the wind was brisk. However before Mr Mondle had got four steps from his cabin door, she struck our ship with her cutwater right in the middle of his bed and cabin and ran it up to the combings of the quarter-deck hatchway and above three feet below water, and in a minute there was not a bit of wood to be seen where Mr Mondle's cabin stood; and he was so near being killed that some of the splinters tore his face. As Mr Mondle must inevitably have perished from this accident had he not been alarmed in the very extraordinary way I have related, I could not help regarding this as an awful interposition of Providence for his preservation. The two ships for some time swung alongside of each other, for ours being a fire-ship, our grappling-irons caught the *Lynne* every way and the yards and rigging went at an astonishing rate. Our ship was in such a shocking condition that we all thought she would instantly go down, and everyone ran for their lives and got as well as they could on board the *Lynne*; but our lieutenant being the aggressor, he never quitted the ship. However when we found she did not sink immediately the captain came on board again and encouraged our people to return and try to save her. Many on this came back, but some would not venture. Some of the ships in the fleet, seeing our situation, immediately sent their boats to our assistance, but it took us the whole day to save the ship with all their help. And by using every possible means, particularly strapping her together with many hawsers and putting a great quantity of tallow below water where she was damaged, she was kept together: but it was well we did not meet with any gales of wind or we must have gone to pieces, for we were in such a crazy condition that we had ships to attend us till we arrived at Belle-Isle, the place of our destination, and then we had all things taken out of the ship and she was properly repaired. This escape of Mr Mondle, which he as well as myself always considered as a singular act of Providence, I believe had a great influence on his life and conduct ever afterwards.

When we had refitted our ship and all things were in

readiness for attacking the place, the troops on board the transport were ordered to disembark, and my master, as a junior captain, had a share in the command of the landing. This was on 8 April. The French were drawn up on the shore and had made every disposition to oppose the landing of our men, only a small part of them this day being able to effect it; most of them, after fighting with great bravery, were cut off, and General Crawford with a number of others were taken prisoners. In this day's engagement we had also our lieutenant killed.

On 21 April we renewed our efforts to land the men while all the men-of-war were stationed along the shore to cover it, and fired at the French batteries and breastworks from early in the morning till about four o'clock in the evening, when our soldiers effected a safe landing. They immediately attacked the French, and after a sharp encounter forced them from the batteries. Before the enemy retreated they blew up several of them, lest they should fall into our hands. Our men now proceeded to besiege the citadel and my master was ordered on shore to superintend the landing of all the materials necessary for carrying on the siege, in which service I mostly attended him. While I was there I went about to different parts of the island, and one day particularly my curiosity almost cost me my life. I wanted very much to see the mode of charging the mortars and letting off the shells and for that purpose I went to an English battery that was but a very few yards from the walls of the citadel. There indeed I had an opportunity of completely gratifying myself in seeing the whole operation, and that not without running a very great risk, both from the English shells that burst while I was there, but likewise from those of the French. One of the largest of their shells bursted within nine or ten yards of me: there was a single rock close by, about the size of a butt, and I got instant shelter under it in time to avoid the fury of the shell. Where it burst the earth was torn in such a manner that two or three butts might easily have gone into the hole it made, and it threw great quantities of stones and dirt to a considerable distance. Three shots were also fired at me and another boy who was along with me; one of them in particular seemed:

'Wing'd with red lightning and impetuous rage',

for with a most dreadful sound it hissed close by me and struck a rock at a little distance which it shattered to pieces. When I saw what perilous circumstances I was in I attempted to return the nearest way I could find and thereby I got between the English and French sentinels. An English sergeant who commanded the outposts, seeing me and surprised how I came there (which was by stealth along the seashore), reprimanded me very severely for it and instantly took the sentinel off his post into custody for his negligence in suffering me to pass the lines. While I was in this situation I observed at a little distance a French horse belonging to some islanders, which I thought I would now mount for the greater expedition of getting off. Accordingly I took some cord which I had about me, and making a kind of bridle of it I put it round the horse's head and the tame beast suffered me to tie him thus and mount him. As soon as I was on the horse's back I began to kick and beat him and try every means to make him go quick, but all to very little purpose: I could not drive him out of a slow pace. While I was creeping along, still within reach of the enemy's shot, I met with a servant well mounted on an English horse. I immediately stopped, and crying, told him my case, and begged of him to help me, and this he effec-tually did; for having a fine large whip, he began to lash my horse with it so severely that he set off full speed with me towards the sea, while I was quite unable to hold or manage him. In this manner I went along till I came to a craggy precipice. I now could not stop my horse, and my mind was filled with apprehensions of my deplorable fate should he go down the precipice, which he appeared fully disposed to do: I therefore thought I had better throw myself off him at once, which I did immediately with a great deal of dexterity and fortunately escaped unhurt. As soon as I found myself at liberty I made the best of my way for the ship, determined I would not be so foolhardy again in a hurry.

We continued to besiege the citadel till June, when it surrendered. During the siege I have counted above sixty shells and carcasses in the air at once. When this place was taken I went through the citadel, and in the bombproofs under it which were cut in the solid rock, and I thought it a surprising place, both for strength and building: notwithstanding which our shots and shells had made amazing devastation and ruinous heaps all around it.

CHAPTER SIX

Hope and Despair

AFTER our ship was fitted out again for service, in September she went to Guernsey, where I was very glad to see my old hostess, who was now a widow, and my former little charming companion, her daughter. I spent some time here very happily with them till October, when we had orders to repair to Portsmouth. We parted from each other with a great deal of affection, and I promised to return soon and see them again, not knowing what all-powerful fate had determined for me. Our ship having arrived at Portsmouth, we went into the harbour and remained there till the latter end of November, when we heard great talk about peace, and to our very great joy in the beginning of December we had orders to go up to London with our ship to be paid off. We received this news with loud huzzas and every other demonstration of gladness, and nothing but mirth was to be seen throughout every part of the ship. I too was not without my share of the general joy on this occasion. I thought now of nothing but being freed and working for myself, and thereby getting money to enable me to get a good education: for I always had a great desire to be able at least to read and write, and while I was on ship-board I had endeavoured to improve myself in both. While I was in the *Ætna* particularly, the captain's clerk taught me to write, and gave me a smattering of arithmetic as far as the rule of three. There was also one Daniel Queen, about forty years of age, a man very well educated, who messed with me on board this ship, and he likewise dressed and attended the captain. Fortunately this man soon became very much attached to me and took very great pains to instruct me in many things. He taught me to shave and dress hair a little and also to read in the Bible, explaining many passages to me which I did not comprehend. I was wonderfully suprised to see the laws and rules of my country written almost exactly here, a circumstance which I believe tended to impress our manners and customs more deeply on my memory. I used to tell him of this resemblance, and many a time we have sat up the whole night together at this employment. In short, he was like a father to me, and some even used to call me after his name; they also styled me the black Christian. Indeed I almost loved him with the affection of a son. Many things I have denied myself that he might have them, and when I used to play at marbles or any other game and won a few halfpence, or got any little money, which I sometimes did, for shaving anyone, I used to buy him a little sugar or tobacco, as far as my stock of money would go. He used to say that he and I never should part, and that when our ship was paid off, as I was as free as himself or any other man on board, he would instruct me in his business by which I might gain a good livelihood. This gave me new life and spirits, and my heart burned within me while I thought the time long till I obtained my freedom. For though my master had not promised it to me, yet besides the assurances I had received that he had no right to detain me, he always treated me with the greatest kindness and reposed in me an unbounded confidence; he even paid attention to my morals, and would never suffer me to deceive him or tell lies, of which he used to tell me the consequences; and that if I did so God would not love me; so that from all this tenderness, I had never once supposed, in all my dreams of freedom, that he would think of detaining me any longer than I wished.

In pursuance of our orders we sailed from Portsmouth for the Thames and arrived at Deptford 10 December, where we cast anchor just as it was high water. The ship was up about half an hour, when my master ordered the barge to be manned, and all in an instant, without having before given me the least reason to suspect anything of the matter, he forced me into the barge, saying I was going to leave him, but he would take care I should not. I was so struck with the unexpectedness of this proceeding that for some time I did not make a reply, only I made an offer to go for my books and chest of clothes, but he swore I should not move out of his sight, and if I did he would cut my throat, at the same time taking his hanger. I began, however, to collect myself, and plucking up courage, I told him I was free and he could not by law serve me so. But this only enraged him the more, and he continued to swear, and said he would soon let me know whether he would or not, and at that instant sprung himself into the barge from the ship to the astonishment and sorrow of all on board. The tide, rather unluckily for me, had just turned downward, so that we quickly fell down the river along with it till we came among some outward-bound West Indiamen, for he was resolved to put me on board the first vessel he could get to receive me. The boat's crew, who pulled against their will, became quite faint, different times, and would have gone ashore, but he would not let them. Some of them strove then to cheer me and told me he could not sell me, which revived me a little, and I still entertained hopes, for as they pulled along he asked some vessels to receive me, but they could not. But just as we had got a little below Gravesend, we came alongside of a ship which was going away the next tide for the West Indies; her name was the *Charming Sally*, Captain James Doran, and my master went on board

and agreed with him for me, and in a little time I was sent
for into the cabin. When I came there Captain Doran
asked me if I knew him; I answered that I did not; 'Then,'
said he, 'you are now my slave'. I told him my master could
not sell me to him, nor to anyone else. 'Why,' said he, 'did
not your master buy you?' I confessed he did. 'But I have
served him,' said I, 'many years, and he has taken all my
wages and prize-money, for I only got one sixpence during
the war; besides this I have been baptized, and by the laws
of the land no man has a right to sell me.' And I added that I
had heard a lawyer and others at different times tell my
master so. They both then said that those people who told
me so were not my friends, but I replied, 'It was very extraordinary that other people did not know the law as well as
they.' Upon this Captain Doran said I talked too much
English, and if I did not behave myself well and be quiet
he had a method on board to make me. I was too well
convinced of his power over me to doubt what he said, and
my former sufferings in the slave-ship presenting themselves
to my mind, the recollection of them made me shudder.
However, before I retired I told them that as I could not
get any right among men here I hoped I should hereafter
in Heaven, and I immediately left the cabin, filled with
resentment and sorrow. The only coat I had with me my
master took away with him, and said if my prize-money
had been £10,000 he had a right to it all and would have
taken it. I had about nine guineas which, during my long
seafaring life, I had scraped together from trifling perquisites and little ventures, and I hid it that instant lest
my master should take that from me likewise, still hoping
that by some means or other I should make my escape to
the shore; and indeed some of my old shipmates told me
not to despair for they would get me back again, and that
as soon as they could get their pay, they would
immediately come to Portsmouth to me, where this ship

was going: but, alas! all my hopes were baffled and the hour of my deliverance was yet far off. My master, having soon concluded his bargain with the captain, came out of the cabin, and he and his people got into the boat and put off; I followed them with aching eyes as long as I could, and when they were out of sight I threw myself on the deck, while my heart was ready to burst with sorrow and anguish.

Soon afterwards, as my new master was going ashore, he called me to him and told me to behave myself well and do the business of the ship the same as any of the rest of the boys and that I should fare the better for it; but I made him no answer. I was then asked if I could swim, and I said, No. However I was made to go under the deck and was well watched. The next tide the ship got under way and soon arrived at the Mother Bank, Portsmouth, where she waited a few days for some of the West India convoy. While I was here I tried every means I could devise amongst the people of the ship to get me a boat from the shore, as there was none suffered to come alongside of the ship, and their own, whenever it was used, was hoisted in again immediately. A sailor on board took a guinea from me on pretence of getting me a boat, and promised me time after time that it was hourly to come off. When he had the watch upon deck I watched also, and looked long enough, but all in vain; I could never see either the boat or my guinea again. And what I thought was still the worst of all, the fellow gave information, as I afterwards found, all the while to the mates of my intention to go off if I could in any way do it; but rogue like, he never told them he had got a guinea from me to procure my escape. However, after we had sailed and his trick was made known to the ship's crew, I had some satisfaction in seeing him detested and despised by them all for his behaviour to me. I was still in hopes that my old shipmates would not forget their promise to come for me to

Portsmouth, and indeed, at last, but not till the day before we sailed, some of them did come there and send me off some oranges and other tokens of their regard. They also sent me word they would come off to me themselves the next day or the day after, and a lady also, who lived in Gosport, wrote to me that she would come and take me out of the ship at the same time. This lady had been once very intimate with my former master: I used to sell and take care of a great deal of property for her in different ships, and in return she always showed great friendship for me, and used to tell my master that she would take me away to live with her: but unfortunately for me, a disagreement soon afterwards took place between them, and she was succeeded in my master's good graces by another lady, who appeared sole mistress of the *Ætna* and mostly lodged on board. I was not so great a favourite with this lady as with the former; she had conceived a pique against me on some occasion when she was on board, and she did not fail to instigate my master to treat me in the manner he did.

However, the next morning, 30 December, the wind being brisk and easterly the *Œolus* frigate, which was to escort the convoy, made a signal for sailing. All the ships then got up their anchors, and before any of my friends had an opportunity to come off to my relief, to my inexpressible anguish our ship had got under way. What tumultuous emotions agitated my soul when the convoy got under sail, and I a prisoner on board, now without hope! I kept my swimming eyes upon the land in a state of unutterable grief, not knowing what to do and despairing how to help myself. While my mind was in this situation the fleet sailed on and in one day's time I lost sight of the wished-for land. In the first expressions of my grief I reproached my fate and wished I had never been born. I was ready to curse the tide that bore us, the gale that wafted my prison, and even the ship that conducted us; and I

called on death to relieve me from the horrors I felt and
dreaded, that I might be in that place

> 'Where slaves are free, and men oppress no more.
> Fool that I was, inur'd so long to pain,
> To trust to hope, or dream of joy again.'

The turbulence of my emotions however naturally gave
way to calmer thoughts, and I soon perceived what fate had
decreed no mortal on earth could prevent. The convoy
sailed on without any accident, with a pleasant gale and
smooth sea for six weeks till February, when one morning
the *Œolus* ran down a brig, one of the convoy, and she
instantly went down and was engulfed in the dark recesses
of the ocean. The convoy was immediately thrown into
great confusion till it was daylight, and the *Œolus* was
illumined with lights to prevent any further mischief. On
13 February 1763, from the mast-head we descried our
destined island Montserrat, and soon after I beheld those

> 'Regions of sorrow, doleful shades, where peace
> And rest can rarely dwell. Hope never comes
> That comes to all, but torture without end
> Still urges.'

At the sight of this land of bondage, a fresh horror ran
through all my frame and chilled me to the heart. My
former slavery now rose in dreadful review to my mind, and
displayed nothing but misery, stripes, and chains; and,
in the first paroxysm of my grief, I called upon God's
thunder and his avenging power to direct the stroke of
death to me rather than permit me to become a slave, and
be sold from lord to lord.

CHAPTER SEVEN

Masters and Slaves

ABOUT the middle of May, when the ship was got ready to sail for England, I all the time believing that Fate's blackest clouds were gathering over my head and expecting their bursting would mix me with the dead, Captain Doran sent for me ashore one morning, and I was told by the messenger that my fate was then determined. With fluttering steps and trembling heart I came to the captain, and found with him one Mr Robert King, a Quaker, and the first merchant in the place. The captain then told me my former master had sent me there to be sold, but that he had desired him to get me the best master he could, as he told him I was a very deserving boy, which Captain Doran said he found to be true; and if he were to stay in the West Indies he would be glad to keep me himself, but he could not venture to take me to London, for he was very sure that when I came there I would leave him. I at that instant burst out a-crying and begged much of him to take me to England with him, but all to no purpose. He told me he had got me the very best master in the whole island, with whom I should be as happy as if I were in England, and for that reason he chose to let him have me, though he could sell me to his own brother-in-law for a great deal more money than what he got from this gentleman. Mr King, my new master, then made a reply, and said the reason he had bought me was on account of my good character; and as he had not the least doubt of my good behaviour I should be very well off with him. He also told me he did not live in the West Indies, but at Philadelphia where he was going soon, and as I understood something of the rules of arithmetic, when we got there he would put me to school and fit me for a clerk. This conversation relieved my mind a little, and I left those gentlemen considerably more at ease in myself than when I came to them; and I was very grateful to Captain Doran, and even to my old master, for the character they had given me, a character which I afterwards found of infinite service to me. I went on board again and took leave of all my shipmates, and the next day the ship sailed. When she weighed anchor I went to the waterside and looked at her with a very wishful and aching heart, and followed her with my eyes and tears until she was totally out of sight. I was so bowed down with grief that I could not hold up my head for many months, and if my new master had not been kind to me I believe I should have died under it at last. And indeed I soon found that he fully deserved the good character which Captain Doran had given me of him, for he possessed a most amiable disposition and temper, and was very charitable and humane. If any of his slaves behaved amiss he did not beat or use them ill, but parted with them. This made them afraid of disobliging him, and as he treated his slaves better than any other man on the island, so he was better and more faithfully served by them in return. By his kind treatment I did at last endeavour to compose myself, and with fortitude, though moneyless, determined to face whatever fate had decreed for me. Mr King soon asked me what I could do, and at the same time said he did not mean to treat me as a common slave. I told him I knew something of seamanship, and could shave and dress hair pretty well; and I could refine wines, which I had learned on shipboard where I had often done it; and that I could write, and understood arithmetic tolerably well as far as the Rule of Three. He then asked me if I knew anything of gauging, and on my answering that I did not, he said one of his clerks should teach me to gauge.

Mr King dealt in all manner of merchandize and kept from one to six clerks. He loaded many vessels in a year, particularly to Philadelphia, where he was born and was connected with a great mercantile house in that city. He had besides many vessels and droggers of different sizes which used to go about the island and others, to collect rum, sugar, and other goods. I understood pulling and managing these boats very well, and this hard work, which was the first that he set me to, in the sugar season used to be my constant employment. I have rowed the boat and slaved at the oars from one hour to sixteen in the twenty-four, during which I had fifteen pence sterling per day to live on, though sometimes only ten pence. However, this was considerably more than was allowed to other slaves that used to work with me, and belonged to other gentlemen on the island: those poor souls had never more than nine pence per day, and seldom more than six pence, from their masters or owners, though they earned them three or four pisterines: for it is a common practice in the West Indies for men to purchase slaves though they have not plantations themselves, in order to let them out to planters and merchants at so much a piece by the day, and they give what allowance they choose out of this produce of their daily work to their slaves for subsistence; this allowance is often very scanty. My master often gave the owners of these slaves two and a half of these pieces per day, and found the poor fellows in victuals himself, because he thought their owners did not feed them well enough according to the work they did. The slaves used to like this very well, and as they knew my master to be a man of feeling, they were always glad to work for him in preference to any other gentleman, some of whom, after they had been paid for these poor people's labour, would not give them their allowance out of it. Many times have I even seen these unfortunate wretches beaten for asking for their pay, and often severely flogged by their owners if they did not bring them their daily or weekly money exactly to the time, though the poor creatures were obliged to wait on the gentlemen they had worked for sometimes for more than half the day before they could get their pay, and this generally on Sundays, when they wanted the time for themselves. In particular, I knew a countryman of mine who once did not bring the weekly money directly that it was earned, and though he brought it the same day to his master, yet he was staked to the ground for this pretended negligence, and was just going to receive a hundred lashes but for a gentleman who begged him off fifty. This poor man was very industrious, and by his frugality had saved so much money by working on shipboard that he had got a white man to buy him a boat, unknown to his master. Some time after he had this little estate the governor wanted a boat to bring his sugar from different parts of the island, and knowing this to be a negro-man's boat he seized upon it for himself, and would not pay the owner a farthing. The man on this went to his master, and complained to him of this act of the governor, but the only satisfaction he received was to be damned very heartily by his master, who asked him how dared any of his negroes to have a boat. If the justly-merited ruin of the governor's fortune could be any gratification to the poor man he had thus robbed, he was not without consolation. Extortion and rapine are poor providers, and some time after this the governor died in the King's Bench in England, as I was told, in great poverty. The last war favoured this poor negro-man, and he found some means to escape from his Christian master. He came to England, where I saw him afterwards several times. Such treatment as this often drives these miserable wretches to despair, and they run away from their masters at the hazard of their lives. Many of them in this place, unable to get their pay when they have earned it, and fearing to be flogged as usual if they return home without it, run away where they can for shelter, and a reward is often offered to bring them in dead or alive. My master used sometimes, in these cases, to agree with their owners and to settle with them himself, and thereby he saved many of them a flogging.

Once, for a few days, I was let out to fit a vessel, and I had no victuals allowed me by either party; at last I told my master of this treatment and he took me away from it. In many of the estates, on the different islands where I used to be sent for rum or sugar, they would not deliver it to me or any other negro; he was therefore obliged to send a white man along with me to those places, and then he used to pay him from six to ten pisterines a day. From being thus employed during the time I served Mr King, in going about the different estates on the island I had all the opportunity I could wish for to see the dreadful usage of the poor men, usage that reconciled me to my situation and made me bless God for the hands into which I had fallen.

I had the good fortune to please my master in every department in which he employed me, and there was scarcely any part of his business or household affairs in which I was not occasionally engaged. I often supplied the place of a clerk in receiving the delivering cargoes to the ships, in tending stores, and delivering goods: and besides this I used to shave and dress my master when convenient, and take care of his horse, and when it was necessary, which was very often, I worked likewise on board of different vessels of his. By these means I became very useful to my master, and saved him, as he used to acknowledge, above a hundred pounds a year. Nor did he scruple to say I was of more advantage to him than any of his clerks, though their usual wages in the West Indies are from sixty to a hundred pounds current a year.

I have sometimes heard it asserted that a negro cannot earn his master the first cost, but nothing can be further from the truth. I suppose nine-tenths of the mechanics throughout the West Indies are negro slaves, and I well know the coopers among them earn two dollars a day, the carpenters the same and oftentimes more, as also the masons, smiths, and fishermen, etc. and I have known many slaves whose masters would not take a thousand pounds current for them. But surely this assertion refutes itself, for if it be true, why do the planters and merchants pay such a price for slaves? And, above all, why do those who make this assertion exclaim the most loudly against the abolition of the slave trade? So much are men blinded, and to such inconsistent arguments are they driven by mistaken interest! I grant, indeed, that slaves are sometimes, by half-feeding, half-clothing, over-working and stripes, reduced so low that they are turned out as unfit for service and left to perish in the woods or expire on a dunghill.

It was very common in several of the islands, particularly in St Kitt's, for the slaves to be branded with the initial letters of their master's name, and a load of heavy iron hooks hung about their necks. Indeed on the most trifling occasions they were loaded with chains, and often instruments of torture were added. The iron muzzle, thumbscrews, etc. are so well known as not to need a description, and were sometimes applied for the slightest faults. I have seen a negro beaten till some of his bones were broken for even letting a pot boil over. It is surprising that usage like this should drive the poor creatures to despair and make them seek refuge in death from those evils which render their lives intolerable – while,

'With shudd'ring horror pale, and eyes aghast,
They view their lamentable lot, and find
No rest!'

This they frequently do. A negro-man on board a
vessel of my master, while I belonged to her, having been
put in irons for some trifling misdemeanour and kept in
that state for some days, being weary of life, took an
opportunity of jumping overboard into the sea; however,
he was picked up without being drowned. Another whose
life was also a burden to him resolved to starve himself to
death, and refused to eat any victuals; this procured him
a severe flogging, and he also, on the first occasion which
offered, jumped overboard at Charleston, but was saved.

Nor is there any greater regard shown to the little
property, than there is to the persons and lives of the
negroes. I have already related an instance or two of
particular oppression out of many which I have witnessed,
but the following is frequent in all the islands. The
wretched field-slaves, after toiling all the day for an unfeeling owner who gives them but little victuals, steal
sometimes a few moments from rest or refreshment to
gather some small portion of grass, according as their
time will admit. This they commonly tie up in a parcel,
(either a bit, worth six pence, or half a bit's-worth) and
bring it to town or to the market to sell. Nothing is more
common than for the white people on this occasion to take
the grass from them without paying for it; and not only so,
but too often also to my knowledge our clerks and many
others at the same time have committed acts of violence
on the poor, wretched, and helpless females, whom I have
seen for hours stand crying to no purpose and get no
redress or pay of any kind. Is not this one common and
crying sin enough to bring down God's judgement on the
islands? He tells us the oppressor and the oppressed are

both in his hands; and if these are not the poor, the broken-hearted, the blind, the captive, the bruised, which our Saviour speaks of, who are they? One of these depredators once in St Eustatia came on board our vessel and bought some fowls and pigs of me, and a whole day after his departure with the things he returned again and wanted his money back: I refused to give it and not seeing my captain on board, he began the common pranks with me, and swore he would even break open my chest and take my money. I therefore expected, as my captain was absent, that he would be as good as his word, and he was just proceeding to strike me, when fortunately a British seaman on board, whose heart had not been debauched by a West India climate, interposed and prevented him. But had the cruel man struck me I certainly should have defended myself at the hazard of my life, for what is life to a man thus oppressed? He went away, however, swearing, and threatened that whenever he caught me on shore he would shoot me, and pay for me afterwards.

The small account in which the life of a negro is held in the West Indies is so universally known that it might seem impertinent to quote the following extract, if some people had not been hardy enough of late to assert that negroes are on the same footing in that respect as Europeans. By the 329th Act, page 125, of the Assembly of Barbadoes, it is enacted 'That if any negro, or other slave, under punishment by his master, or his order, for running away, or any other crime or misdemeanour towards his said master, unfortunately shall suffer in life or member, no person whatsoever shall be liable to a fine, but if any man shall out of *wantonness, or only of bloody-mindedness, or cruel intention, wilfully kill a negro, or other slave, of his own, he shall pay into the public treasury fifteen pounds sterling.*' And it is the same in most, if not all, of the West India islands. Is not this one of the many acts of the islands which call loudly for redress? And do not the assembly which enacted it deserve the appellation of savages and brutes rather than of Christians and men? It is an act at once unmerciful, unjust, and unwise, which for cruelty would disgrace an assembly of those who are called barbarians, and for its injustice and *insanity* would shock the morality and common sense of a Samoyed or a Hottentot.

Shocking as this and many more acts of the bloody West India code at first view appear, how is the iniquity of it heightened when we consider to whom it may be extended! Mr James Tobin, a zealous labourer in the vineyard of slavery, gives an account of a French planter of his acquaintance in the island of Martinique who showed him many mulattoes working in the fields like beasts of burden, and he told Mr Tobin these were all the produce of his own loins! And I myself have known similar instances. Pray, reader, are these sons and daughters of the French planter less his children by being begotten on a black woman? And what must be the virtue of those legislators and the feelings of those fathers, who estimate the lives of their sons, however begotten, at no more than fifteen pounds, though they should be murdered, as the acts says, *out of wantonness and bloody-mindedness*! But is not the slave trade entirely a war with the heart of man? And surely that which is begun by breaking down the barriers of virtue involves in its continuance destruction to every principle, and buries all sentiments in ruin!

I have often seen slaves, particularly those who were meagre, in different islands, put into scales and weighed, and then sold from three pence to six pence or nine pence a pound. My master, however, whose humanity was shocked at this mode, used to sell such by the lump. And at or after a sale it was not uncommon to see negroes taken from their wives, wives taken from their husbands, and children from their parents, and sent off to other islands, and wherever else their merciless lords chose; and probably never more during life to see each other! Oftentimes my heart had bled at these partings, when the friends of the departed have been at the waterside, and with sighs and tears have kept their eyes fixed on the vessel till it went out of sight.

A poor Creole negro I knew well, who, after having been often thus transported from island to island, at last resided in Montserrat. This man used to tell me many melancholy tales of himself. Generally, after he had done working for his master, he used to employ his few leisure moments to go a-fishing. When he had any fish his master would frequently take them from him without paying him, and at other times some other white people would serve him in the same manner. One day he said to me, very movingly, 'Sometimes when a white man take away my fish I go to my master, and he get me my right; and when my master by strength take away my fishes, what me must do? I can't go to anybody to be righted; then,' said the poor man, looking up above, 'I must look up to God Mighty in the top for right'. This artless tale moved me much and I could not help feeling the just causes Moses had in redressing his brother against the Egyptian. I exhorted the man to look up still to the God on the top since there was no redress below. Though I little thought then that I myself should more than once experience such imposition and read the same exhortation hereafter in my own transactions in the islands, and that even this poor man and I should some time after suffer together in the same manner, as shall be related hereafter.

Nor was such usage as this confined to particular places or individuals, for in all the different islands in which I have been (and I have visited no less than fifteen) the treatment of the slaves was nearly the same; so nearly indeed, that the history of an island or even a plantation, with a few such exceptions as I have mentioned, might serve for a history of the whole. Such a tendency has the slave-trade to debauch men's minds and harden them to every feeling of humanity! For I will not suppose that the dealers in slaves are born worse than other men – No, it is the fatality of this mistaken avarice that it corrupts the milk of human kindness and turns it into gall. And had the pursuits of those men been different, they might have been as generous, as tender-hearted and just, as they are unfeeling, rapacious and cruel. Surely this traffic cannot be good, which spreads like a pestilence and taints what it touches! which violates that first natural right of mankind, equality and independency, and gives one man a dominion over his fellows which God could never intend! For it raises the owner to a state as far above man as it depresses the slave below it, and with all the presumption of human pride, sets a distinction between them, immeasurable in extent and endless in duration! Yet how mistaken is the avarice even of the planters! Are slaves more useful by being thus humbled to the condition of brutes than they would be if suffered to enjoy the privileges of men? The freedom which diffuses health and prosperity throughout Britain answers you – No. When you make men slaves you deprive them of half their virtue, you set them in your own conduct an example of fraud, rapine, and cruelty, and compel them to live with you in a state of war, and yet you complain that they are not honest or faithful! You stupefy them with stripes and think it necessary to keep them in a state of ignorance, and yet you assert that they are incapable of learning, that their minds are such a barren soil or moor that culture would be lost on them, and that they come from a climate where nature, though prodigal of her bounties in a degree unknown to yourselves, has left man alone scant and unfinished and incapable of enjoying the treasures she had poured out for him! – An assertion at once

impious and absurd. Why do you use those instruments
of torture? Are they fit to be applied by one rational being
to another? And are ye not struck with shame and mortification to see the partakers of your nature reduced so
low? But above all, are there no dangers attending this
mode of treatment? Are you not hourly in dread of an
insurrection? Nor would it be surprising: for when

> ' – No peace is given
> To us enslav'd, but custody severe;
> And stripes and arbitrary punishment
> Inflicted – What peace can we return?
> But to our power, hostility and hate;
> Untam'd reluctance, and revenge, though slow.
> Yet ever plotting how the conqueror least
> May reap his conquest, and may least rejoice
> In doing what we most in suffering feel.'

But by changing your conduct and treating your slaves as
men every cause of fear would be banished. They would be
faithful, honest, intelligent and vigorous; and peace,
prosperity, and happiness, would attend you.

CHAPTER EIGHT

West Indian Voyages

Some time in the year 1763 kind Providence seemed to appear rather more favourable to me. One of my master's vessels, a Bermudas sloop, about sixty tons, was commanded by one Captain Thomas Farmer, an Englishman, a very alert and active man who gained my master a great deal of money by his good management in carrying passengers from one island to another; but very often his sailors used to get drunk and run away from the vessel, which hindered him in his business very much. This man had taken a liking to me, and many different times begged of my master to let me go a trip with him as a sailor; but he would tell him he could not spare me, though the vessel sometimes could not go for want of hands, for sailors were generally very scarce in the island. However, at last, from necessity or force, my master was prevailed on, though very reluctantly, to let me go with this captain; but he gave great charge to him to take care that I did not run away, for if I did he would make him pay for me. This being the case, the captain had for some time a sharp eye upon me whenever the vessel anchored, and as soon as she returned I was sent for on shore again. Thus was I slaving as it were for life, sometimes at one thing and sometimes at another, so that the captain and I were nearly the most useful men in my master's employment. I also became so useful to the captain on shipboard that many times when he used to ask for me to go with him, though it should be but for twenty-four hours, to some of the islands near us, my master would answer he could not spare me, at which the captain would swear, and would not go the trip, and tell my master I was better to him on board than any three white men he had: for they used to behave ill in many respects, particularly in getting drunk, and then they frequently got the boat stove so as to hinder the vessel from coming back as soon as she might have done. This my master knew very well, and at last by the captain's constant entreaties, after I had been several times with him, one day to my great joy my master told me the captain would not let him rest, and asked me whether I would go aboard as a sailor, or stay on shore and mind the stores, for he could not bear any longer to be plagued in this manner. I was very happy at this proposal for I immediately thought I might in time stand some chance by being on board to get a little money or possibly make my escape if I should be used ill; I also expected to get better food and in greater abundance, for I had felt much hunger oftentimes, though my master treated his slaves, as I have observed, uncommonly well. I therefore without hesitation answered him that I would go and be a sailor if he pleased. Accordingly I was ordered on board directly. Nevertheless, between the vessel and the shore when she was in port I had little or no rest, as my master always wished to have me along with him. Indeed he was a very pleasant gentleman and but for my expectations on shipboard I should not have thought of leaving him. But the captain liked me also very much and I was entirely his right-hand man. I did all I could to deserve this favour and in return I received better treatment from him than any other I believe ever met with in the West Indies in my situation.

After I had been sailing for some time with this captain, at length I endeavoured to try my luck and commence

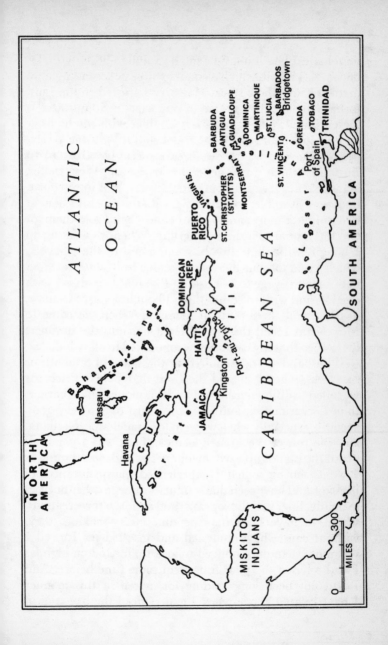

merchant. I had but a very small capital to begin with, for one single half bit, which is equal to three pence in England, made up my whole stock. However I trusted to the Lord to be with me, and at one of our trips to St Eustatia, a Dutch island, I bought a glass tumbler with my half bit, and when I came to Montserrat I sold it for a bit, or six-pence. Luckily we made several successive trips to St Eustatia (which was a general mart for the West Indies, about twenty leagues from Montserrat), and in our next, finding my tumbler so profitable, with this one bit I bought two tumblers more; and when I came back I sold them for two bits, equal to a shilling sterling. When we went again I bought with these two bits four more of these glasses, which I sold for four bits on our return to Montserrat: and in our next voyage to St Eustatia I bought two glasses with one bit, and with the other three I bought a jug of Geneva, nearly about three pints in measure. When we came to Montserrat I sold the gin for eight bits and the tumblers for two, so that my capital now amounted in all to a dollar, well husbanded and acquired in the space of a month or six weeks, when I blessed the Lord that I was so rich. As we sailed to different islands I laid this money out in various things occasionally, and it used to turn out to very good account, especially when we went to Guadeloupe, Grenada, and the rest of the French islands. Thus was I going all about the islands upwards of four years, and ever trading as I went, during which I experienced many instances of ill usage and have seen many injuries done to other negroes in our dealings with Europeans: and amidst our recreations, when we have been dancing and merry-making, they, without cause, have molested and insulted us. Indeed I was more than once obliged to look up to God on high, as I had advised the poor fisherman some time before. And I had not been long trading for myself in this manner I have related above when I experienced the like trial in company with him as follows: This man being used to the water, was upon an emergency put on board of us by his master to work as another hand on a voyage to Santa Cruz, and at our sailing he had brought his little all for a venture, which consisted of six bits' worth of limes and oranges in a bag; I had also my whole stock, which was about twelve bits' worth of the same kind of goods, separate in two bags, for we had heard these fruits sold well in that island. When we came there, in some little convenient time he and I went ashore with our fruits to sell them, but we had scarcely landed when we were met by two white men, who presently took our three bags from us. We could not at first guess what they meant to do, and for some time we thought they were jesting with us, but they too soon let us know otherwise, for they took our ventures immediately to a house hard by, and adjoining the fort, while we followed all the way begging of them to give us our fruits, but in vain. They not only refused to return them, but swore at us and threatened if we did not immediately depart they would flog us well. We told them these three bags were all we were worth in the world, and that we brought them with us to sell when we came from Montserrat, and showed them the vessel. But this was rather against us, as they now saw we were strangers as well as slaves. They still therefore swore and desired us to be gone, and even took sticks to beat us, while we, seeing they meant what they said, went off in the greatest confusion and despair. Thus in the very minute of gaining more by three times than I ever did by any venture in my life before, was I deprived of every farthing I was worth. An insupportable misfortune! but how to help ourselves we knew not. In our consternation we went to the commanding officer of the fort and told him how we had been served by some of his people, but we obtained not the least redress: he answered our complaints only by a volley of imprecations against us, and immediately took a horse-whip in order to chastise us, so that we were obliged to turn out much faster than we came in. I now, in the agony of distress and indignation, wished that the ire of God in his forked lightning might transfix these cruel oppressors among the dead. Still however we persevered, went back again to the house, and begged and besought them again and again for our fruits, till at last some other people that were in the house asked if we would be contented if they kept one bag and gave us the other two. We, seeing no remedy whatever, consented to this, and they, observing one bag to have both kinds of fruit in it, which belonged to my companion, kept that; and the other two, which were mine, they gave us back. As soon as I got them I ran as fast as I could, and got the first negro man I could to help me off; my companion, however, stayed a little longer to plead; he told them the bag they had was his, and likewise all that he was worth in the world, but this was of no avail and he was obliged to return without it. The poor old man, wringing his hands, cried bitterly for his loss, and indeed he then did look up to God on high, which so moved me with pity for him that I gave him nearly one-third of my fruits. We then proceeded to the markets to sell them, and Providence was more favourable to us than we could have expected, for we sold our fruits uncommonly well; I got for mine about thirty-seven bits. Such a surprising reverse of fortune in so short a space of time seemed like a dream to me, and proved no small encouragement for me to trust the Lord in any situation. My captain afterwards frequently used to take my part, and get me my right when I have been plundered or used ill by these tender Christian depredators, among whom I have shuddered to observe the unceasing blasphemous execrations which are wantonly thrown out by persons of all ages and conditions, not only without occasion, but even as if they were indulgences and pleasure.

At one of our trips to St Kitt's I had eleven bits of my own, and my friendly captain lent me five bits more with which I bought a Bible. I was very glad to get this book, which I scarcely could meet with anywhere. I think there was none sold in Montserrat, and much to my grief, from being forced out of the *Ætna* in the manner I have related, my Bible, and the Guide to the Indians, the two books I loved above all others, were left behind.

While I was in this place, St Kitt's, a very curious imposition on human nature took place: A white man wanted to marry in the church a free black woman that had land and slaves in Montserrat, but the clergyman told him it was against the law of the place to marry a white and a black in the church. The man then asked to be married on the water, to which the parson consented, and the two lovers went in one boat and the parson and clerk in another, and thus the ceremony was performed. After this the loving pair came on board our vessel and my captain treated them extremely well and brought them safe to Montserrat.

The reader cannot but judge of the irksomeness of this situation to a mind like mine in being daily exposed to new hardships and impositions after having seen many better days and having been as it were in a state of freedom and plenty; added to which, every part of the world I had hitherto been in seemed to me a paradise in comparison of the West Indies. My mind was therefore hourly replete with inventions and thoughts of being freed, and if possible by honest and honourable means, for I always remembered the old adage, and I trust it has ever been my ruling principle, that honesty is the best policy; and likewise that other golden precept – to do unto all men as I would they should do unto me. However, as I was from early years a predestinarian, I thought whatever fate had determined must ever come to pass, and therefore if ever it were my lot to be freed nothing could prevent me, although I should at present see no means or hope to obtain my freedom; on the other hand, if it were my fate not to be freed I never should be so, and all my endeavours for that purpose would be fruitless. In the midst of these thoughts I therefore looked up with prayers anxiously to God for my liberty, and at the same time I used every honest means, and endeavoured all that was possible on my part to obtain it. In process of time I became master of a few pounds and in a fair way of making more, which my friendly captain knew very well; this occasioned him sometimes to take liberties with me, but whenever he treated me waspishly I used plainly to tell him my mind and that I would die before I would be imposed on as other negroes were and that to me life had lost its relish when liberty was gone. This I said although I foresaw my then wellbeing or future hopes of freedom (humanly speaking) depended on this man. However, as he could not bear the thoughts of my not sailing with him, he always became mild on my threats. I therefore continued with him, and from my great attention to his orders and his business I gained him credit, and through his kindness to me I at last procured my liberty. While I thus went on, filled with the thoughts of freedom and resisting oppression as well as I was able, my life hung daily in suspense, particularly in the surfs I have formerly mentioned, as I could not swim. These are extremely violent throughout the West Indies, and I was ever exposed to their howling rage and devouring fury in all the islands. I have seen them strike and toss a boat right up on end and maim several on board. Once in the Grenada islands, when I and about eight others were pulling a large boat with two puncheons of water in it, a surf struck us and drove the boat and all in it about half a stone's throw among some trees and above the high water mark. We were obliged to get all the assistance we could from the nearest estate to mend the boat and launch it into the water again. At Montserrat one night, in pressing hard to get off the shore on board, the punt was overset with us four times; the first time I was very near being drowned; however the jacket I had on kept me up above the water a little space of time, while I called on a man near me who was a good swimmer and told him I could not swim; he then made haste to me, and just as I was sinking he caught hold of me and brought me to sounding, and then he went and brought the punt also. As soon as we had turned the water out of her, lest we should be used ill for being absent we attempted again three times more, and as often the horrid surfs served us as at first; but at last, the fifth time we attempted, we gained our point at the imminent hazard of our lives. One day also, at Old Road in Montserrat, our captain and three men besides myself were going in a large canoe in quest of rum and sugar when a single surf tossed the canoe an amazing distance from the water and some of us even a stone's throw from each other: most of us were very much bruised, so that I and many more often said, and really thought, that there was not such another place under the heavens as this. I longed therefore much to leave it and daily wished to see my master's promise performed of going to Philadelphia. While we lay in this place a very cruel thing happened on board of our sloop which filled me with horror, though I found afterwards such practices were frequent. There was a very clever and decent free young mulatto-man who sailed a long time with us: he had a free woman for his wife, by whom he had a child, and she was then living on shore and all very happy. Our captain and mate and other people on board and several elsewhere, even the natives of Bermudas, all knew this young man from a child that he was always free, and no one had ever claimed him as their property: however, as might too often overcomes right in these parts, it happened that a Bermudas captain whose vessel lay there for a few days in the road came on board of us, and seeing the mulatto-man, whose name was Joseph Clipson, he told him he was not free and that he had orders from his master to bring him to Bermudas. The poor man could not believe the captain to be in earnest, but he was very soon undeceived, his men laying violent hands on him: and although he showed a certificate of his being born free in St Kitt's, and most people on board knew that he served his time to boat-building and always passed for a free man, yet he was taken forcibly out of our vessel. He then asked to be carried ashore before the secretary or magistrates, and these infernal invaders of human rights promised him he should; but instead of that, they carried him on board of the other vessel, and the next day, without giving the poor man any hearing on shore or suffering him even to see his wife or child, he was carried away and probably doomed never more to see them again. Nor was this the only instance of this kind of barbarity I was a witness to. I have since often seen in Jamaica and other islands free men, whom I have known in America, thus villainously trepanned and held in bondage. I have heard of two similar practices even in Philadelphia, and were it not for the benevolence of the Quakers in that city many of the sable race who now breathe the air of liberty would, I believe, be groaning indeed under some planter's chains. These things opened my mind to a new scene of horror to which I had been before a stranger. Hitherto I had thought only slavery dreadful, but the state of a free negro appeared to me now equally so at least, and in some respects even worse, for they live in constant alarm for their liberty; and even this is but nominal, for they are universally insulted and plundered without the possibility of redress; for such is the equity of the West Indian laws, that no free negro's evidence will be admitted in their courts of justice. In this situation is it surprising that slaves, when mildly treated, should prefer even the misery of slavery to such a mockery of freedom? I was now completely disgusted with the West Indies and thought I never should be entirely free until I had left them.

I determined to make every exertion to obtain my freedom and to return to Old England. For this purpose I thought a knowledge of navigation might be of use to me, for though I did not intend to run away unless I should be ill used, yet in such a case, if I understood navigation, I might attempt my escape in our sloop, which was one of the swiftest sailing vessels in the West Indies, and I could be at no loss for hands to join me: and if I should make this attempt, I had intended to have gone for England; but this, as I said, was only to be in the event of my meeting with any ill-usage. I therefore employed the mate of our vessel to teach me navigation, for which I agreed to give him twenty-four dollars, and actually paid him part of the money down; though when the captain some time after came to know that the mate was to have such a sum for teaching me, he rebuked him and said it was a shame for him to take any money from me. However, my progress in this useful art was much retarded by the constancy of our work. Had I wished to run away I did not want opportunities which frequently presented themselves, and particularly at one time, soon after this. When we were at the island of Guadeloupe there was a large fleet of merchant-men bound for Old France, and seamen then being very scarce, they gave from fifteen to twenty pounds a man for the run. Our mate and all the white sailors left our vessel on this account, and went on board of the French ships. They would have had me also to go with them, for they regarded me and they swore to protect me if I would go: and as the fleet was to sail the next day I really believe I could have got safe to Europe at that time. However, as my master was kind, I would not attempt to leave him, and remembering the old maxim, that 'honesty is the best policy', I suffered them to go without me. Indeed my captain was much afraid of my leaving him and the vessel at that time, as I had so fair an opportunity: but I thank God, this fidelity turned out much to my advantage hereafter, when I did not in the least think of it, and made me so much in favour with the captain that he used now and then to teach me some parts of navigation himself: but some of our passengers and others, seeing this, found much fault with him for it, saying it was a very dangerous thing to let a negro know navigation; thus I was hindered again in my pursuits. About the latter end of the year 1764 my master bought a larger sloop, called the *Providence*, about seventy or eighty tons, of which my captain had the command. I went with him into this vessel, and we took a load of new slaves for Georgia and Charleston. My master now left me entirely to the captain, though he still wished for me to be with him; but I, who always much wished to lose sight of the West Indies, was not a little rejoiced at the thoughts of seeing any other country. Therefore, relying on the goodness of my captain, I got ready all the little venture I could, and when the vessel was ready we sailed to my great joy. When we got to our destined places, Georgia and Charleston I expected I should have an opportunity of selling my little property to advantage: but here, particularly in Charleston, I met with buyers, white men, who imposed on me as in other places. Notwithstanding, I was resolved to have fortitude, thinking no lot or trial is too hard when kind Heaven is the rewarder. We soon got loaded again and returned to Montserrat, and there, amongst the rest of the islands, I sold my goods well; and in this manner I continued trading during the year 1764, meeting with various scenes of imposition, as usual. After this, my master fitted out his vessel for Philadelphia in the year 1765, and during the time we were loading her and getting ready for the voyage I worked with redoubled alacrity from the hope of getting money enough by these voyages to buy my freedom in time, if it should please God; and also to see the town of Philadelphia, which I had heard a great deal about for some years past; besides which, I had always longed to prove my master's promise the first day I came to him. In the midst of these elevated ideas, and while I was about getting my little merchandize in readiness, on Sunday my master sent for me to his house. When I came there I found him and the captain together, and on my going in, I was struck with astonishment at his telling me he had heard that I meant to run away from him when I got to Philadelphia: 'And therefore,' said he, 'I must sell you again: you cost me a great deal of money, no less than forty pounds sterling, and it will not do to lose so much. You are a valuable fellow,' continued he; 'and I can get any day for you one hundred guineas from many gentlemen in this island.' And then he told me of Captain Doran's brother-in-law, a severe master, who ever wanted to buy me to make me his overseer. My captain also said he could get much more than a hundred guineas for me in Carolina. This I knew to be a fact, for the gentleman that wanted to buy me came off several times on board of us, and spoke to me to live with him, and said he would use me well. When I asked what work he would put me to he said, as I was a sailor, he would make me a captain of one of his rice vessels. But I refused, and fearing, at the same time, but a sudden turn I saw in the captain's temper, he might mean to sell me, I told the gentleman I would not live with him on any condition, and that I certainly would run away with his vessel: but he said he did not fear that as he would catch me again, and then he told me how cruelly he would serve me if I should do so. My captain, however, gave him to understand that I knew something of navigation: so he thought better of it, and to my great joy he went away. I now told my master I did not say I would run away in Philadelphia, neither did I mean it, as he did not use me

ill, nor yet the captain: for if they did I certainly would
have made some attempts before now; but as I thought
that if it were God's will I ever should be freed it would be
so, and on the contrary, if it was not his will it would not
happen, so I hoped if ever I were freed, whilst I was used
well it should be by honest means; but as I could not help
myself, he must do as he pleased; I could only hope and
trust to the God of Heaven, and at that instant my mind
was big with inventions and full of schemes to escape. I
then appealed to the captain whether he ever saw any sign
of my making the least attempt to run away, and asked him
if I did not always come on board according to the time for
which he gave me liberty, and more particularly, when all
our men left us at Guadeloupe and went on board of the
French fleet and advised me to go with them, whether I
might not, and that he could not have got me again. To
my no small surprise and very great joy, the captain confirmed every syllable that I had said, and even more; for
he said he had tried different times to see if I would make
any attempt of this kind, both at St Eustatia and in
America, and he never found that I made the smallest;
but on the contrary, I always came on board according to
his orders, and he did really believe, if I ever meant to
run away, that as I could never have had a better opportunity, I would have done it the night the mate and all the
people left our vessel at Guadeloupe. The captain then
informed my master, who had been thus imposed on by our
mate, though I did not know who was my enemy, the
reason the mate had for imposing this lie upon him; which
was, because I had acquainted the captain of the provisions
the mate had given away or taken out of the vessel. This
speech of the captain was like life to the dead to me, and
instantly my soul glorified God; and still more so on
hearing my master immediately say that I was a sensible
fellow and he never did intend to use me as a common slave,

and that but for the entreaties of the captain and his character of me he would not have let me go from the stores about as I had done; that also, in so doing, he thought by carrying one little thing or other to different places to sell I might make money. That he also intended to encourage me in this by crediting me with half a puncheon of rum and half a hogshead of sugar at a time, so that from being careful, I might have money enough, in some time, to purchase my freedom; and, when that was the case, I might depend upon it he would let me have it for forty pounds sterling money, which was only the same price he gave for me. This sound gladdened my poor heart beyond measure; though indeed it was no more than the very idea I had formed in my mind of my master long before, and I immediately made him this reply: 'Sir, I always had that very thought of you, indeed I had, and that made me so diligent in serving you.' He then gave me a large piece of silver coin such as I never had seen or had before, and told me to get ready for the voyage, and he would credit me with a tierce of sugar and another of rum; he also said that he had two amiable sisters in Philadelphia from whom I might get some necessary things. Upon this my noble captain desired me to go aboard, and knowing the African mettle, he charged me not to say anything of this matter to anybody, and he promised that the lying mate should not go with him any more. This was a change indeed; in the same hour to feel the most exquisite pain, and in the turn of a moment the fullest joy. It caused in me such sensations as I was only able to express in my looks; my heart was so overpowered with gratitude that I could have kissed both of their feet. When I left the room I immediately went, or rather flew, to the vessel, which being loaded, my master, as good as his word, trusted me with a tierce of rum and another of sugar when we sailed, and arrived safe at the elegant town of Philadelphia. I soon sold my goods here pretty well, and in this charming place I found everything plentiful and cheap.

While I was in this place a very extraordinary occurrence befell me. I had been told one evening of a *wise* woman, a Mrs Davis, who revealed secrets, foretold events, etc. I put little faith in this story at first, as I could not conceive that any mortal could foresee the future disposals of Providence, nor did I believe in any other revelation than that of the Holy Scriptures; however, I was greatly astonished at seeing this woman in a dream that night, though a person I never before beheld in my life; this made such an impression on me that I could not get the idea the next day out of my mind, and I then became as anxious to see her as I was before indifferent; accordingly in the evening after we left off working I inquired where she lived, and being directed to her, to my inexpressible surprise beheld the very woman in the very same dress she appeared to me to wear in the vision. She immediately told me I had dreamed of her the preceding night, related to me many things that had happened with a correctness that astonished me, and finally told me I should not be long a slave: this was the more agreeable news, as I believed it the more readily from her having so faithfully related the past incidents of my life. She said I should be twice in very great danger of my life within eighteen months, which if I escaped, I should afterwards go on well; so, giving me her blessing, we parted. After staying here some time till our vessel was loaded and I had bought in my little traffic, we sailed from this agreeable spot for Montserrat once more to encounter the raging surfs.

CHAPTER NINE

Free Man

EVERY day now brought me nearer to my freedom, and I was impatient till we proceeded again to sea, that I might have an opportunity of getting a sum large enough to purchase it. I was not long ungratified, for in the beginning of 1766 my master bought another sloop, named the *Nancy*, the largest I had ever seen. She was partly laden, and was to proceed to Philadelphia. Our captain had his choice of three, and I was well pleased he chose this, which was the largest, for from his having a large vessel I had more room and could carry a larger quantity of goods with me. Accordingly, when we had delivered our old vessel, the *Prudence*, and completed the lading of the *Nancy*, having made near 300 per cent by four barrels of pork I brought from Charleston, I laid in as large a cargo as I could, trusting to God's providence to prosper my undertaking. With these views I sailed for Philadelphia.

We arrived safe and in good time at Philadelphia, and I sold my goods there chiefly to the Quakers. They always appeared to be a very honest discreet sort of people, and never attempted to impose on me; I therefore liked them, and ever after chose to deal with them in preference to any others. One Sunday morning while I was here, as I was going to church, I chanced to pass a meeting-house. The doors being open, and the house full of people, it excited my curiosity to go in. When I entered the house, to my great surprise, I saw a very tall woman standing in the midst of them, speaking in an audible voice something which I could not understand. Having never seen anything of this kind before, I stood and stared about me for some time, wondering at this odd scene. As soon as it was over I took an opportunity to make inquiry about the place and people, when I was informed they were called Quakers. I particularly asked what that woman I saw in the midst of them had said, but none of them were pleased to satisfy me; so I quitted them, and soon after, as I was returning, I came to a church crowded with people: the churchyard was full likewise, and a number of people were even mounted on ladders, looking in at the windows. I thought this a strange sight, as I had never seen churches, either in England or the East Indies, crowded in this manner before. I therefore made bold to ask some people the meaning of all this, and they told me the Rev. Mr George Whitefield was preaching. I had often heard of this gentleman, and had wished to see and hear him; but I had never before had an opportunity. I now therefore resolved to gratify myself with the sight and pressed in amidst the multitude. When I got into the church I saw this pious man exhorting the people with the greatest fervour and earnestness, and sweating as much as I ever did while in slavery on Montserrat beach. I was very much struck and impressed with this; I thought it strange I had never seen divines exert themselves in this manner before, and I was no longer at a loss to account for the thin congregations they preached to.

When we had discharged our cargo here and were loaded again, we left this fruitful land once more and set sail for Montserrat. My traffic had hitherto succeeded so well with me that I thought, by selling my goods when we arrived at Montserrat, I should have enough to purchase my freedom. But as soon as our vessel arrived there, my master came on board and gave orders for us to go to St Eustatia

and discharge our cargo there, and from thence proceed
for Georgia. I was much disappointed at this, but thinking,
as usual, it was of no use to encounter with the decrees of
fate, I submitted without repining and we went to St
Eustatia. After we had discharged our cargo there we took
in a live cargo, as we call a cargo of slaves. Here I sold my
goods tolerably well, but not being able to lay out all my
money in this small island to as much advantage as in
many other places, I laid out only part, and the remainder
I brought away with me neat. We sailed from hence for
Georgia, and I was glad when we got there though I had
not much reason to like the place from my last adventure
in Savannah; but I longed to get back to Montserrat and
procure my freedom, which I expected to be able to
purchase when I returned. As soon as we arrived here I
waited on my careful doctor, Mr Brady, to whom I made
the most grateful acknowledgments in my power for his
former kindness and attention during my illness. While we
were here an odd circumstance happened to the captain
and me, which disappointed us both a good deal. A
silversmith, whom we had brought to this place some
voyages before, agreed with the captain to return with us
to the West Indies and promised at the same time to give
the captain a great deal of money, having pretended to
take a liking to him, and being, as we thought, very rich.
But while we stayed to load our vessel this man was taken
ill in a house where he worked, and in a week's time became
very bad. The worse he grew the more he used to speak
of giving the captain what he had promised him, so that
he expected something considerable from the death of
this man, who had no wife or child, and he attended him
day and night. I used also to go with the captain at his
own desire, to attend him, especially when we saw there
was no appearance of his recovery: and in order to recompense me for my trouble, the Captain promised me ten

pounds when he should get the man's property. I thought this would be of great service to me, although I had nearly money enough to purchase my freedom if I should get safe this voyage to Montserrat. In this expectation I laid out above eight pounds of my money for a suit of superfine clothes to dance with at my freedom, which I hoped was then at hand. We still continued to attend this man and were with him even on the last day he lived till very late at night, when we went on board. After we were got to bed, about one or two o'clock in the morning, the captain was sent for and informed the man was dead. On this he came to my bed, and waking me, informed me of it, and desired me to get up and procure a light, and immediately go to him. I told him I was very sleepy and wished he would take somebody else with him; or else, as the man was dead and could want no further attendance, to let all things remain as they were till the next morning. 'No, no,' said he, 'we will have the money tonight, I cannot wait till tomorrow, so let us go.' Accordingly I got up and struck a light, and away we both went and saw the man as dead as we could wish. The captain said he would give him a grand burial in gratitude for the promised treasure, and desired that all the things belonging to the deceased might be brought forth. Amongst others, there was a nest of trunks of which he had kept the keys whilst the man was ill, and when they were produced we opened them with no small eagerness and expectation; and as there were a great number within one another, with much impatience we took them one out of the other. At last, when we came to the smallest and had opened it, we saw it was full of papers, which we supposed to be notes, at the sight of which our hearts leapt for joy, and that instant the captain, clapping his hands, cried out, 'Thank God, here it is.' But when we took up the trunk and began to examine the supposed treasure and long-looked-for bounty, (alas! alas!

how uncertain and deceitful are all human affairs!) what
had we found! While we thought we were embracing a
substance we grasped an empty nothing. The whole amount
that was in the nest of trunks was only one dollar and a half,
and all that the man possessed would not pay for his coffin.
Our sudden and exquisite joy was now succeeded by as
sudden and exquisite pain, and my captain and I exhibited
for some time most ridiculous figures – pictures of chagrin
and disappointment! We went away greatly mortified
and left the deceased to do as well as he could for himself
as we had taken so good care of him when alive for nothing.
We set sail once more for Montserrat and arrived there safe,
but much out of humour with our friend the silversmith.
When we had unladen the vessel and I had sold my venture,
finding myself master of about forty-seven pounds I
consulted my true friend, the captain, how I should proceed
in offering my master the money for my freedom. He told
me to come on a certain morning, when he and my master
would be at breakfast together. Accordingly, on that
morning I went and met the captain there as he had
appointed. When I went in I made my obeisance to my
master, and with money in my hand and many fears
in my heart I prayed him to be as good as his offer to
me, when he was pleased to promise me my freedom as
soon as I could purchase it. This speech seemed to con-
found him; he began to recoil: and my heart that instant
sunk within me. 'What,' said he, 'give you your freedom?
Why, where did you get the money? Have you got forty
pounds sterling?' 'Yes, sir,' I answered. 'How did you get
it?' replied he. I told him very honestly. The captain then
said he knew I got the money very honestly and with much
industry, and that I was particularly careful. On which my
master replied I got money much faster than he did, and
said he would not have made me the promise he did if he
had thought I should have got money so soon. 'Come, come,'

said my worthy captain, clapping my master on the back, 'Come, Robert, (which was his name) I think you must let him have his freedom; you have laid your money out very well; you have received good interest for it all this time, and here is now the principal at last. I know Gustavus has earned you more than an hundred a year, and he will still save you money, as he will not leave you. Come, Robert, take the money.' My master then said he would not be worse than his promise, and taking the money, told me to go to the Secretary at the Register Office and get my manumission drawn up. These words of my master were like a voice from Heaven to me. In an instant all my trepidation was turned into unutterable bliss, and I most reverently bowed myself with gratitude, unable to express my feelings but by the overflowing of my eyes, while my true and worthy friend, the captain, congratulated us both with a peculiar degree of heartfelt pleasure. As soon as the first transports of my joy were over, and that I had expressed my thanks to these my worthy friends in the best manner I was able, I rose with a heart full of affection and reverence and left the room, in order to obey my master's joyful mandate of going to the Register Office. As I was leaving the house I called to mind the words of the Psalmist, in the 126th Psalm, and like him, 'I glorified God in my heart, in whom I trusted.' These words had been impressed on my mind from the very day I was forced from Deptford to the present hour, and I now saw them, as I thought, fulfilled and verified. My imagination was all rapture as I flew to the Register Office, and in this respect, like the apostle Peter, (whose deliverance from prison was so sudden and extraordinary, that he thought he was in a vision) I could scarcely believe I was awake. Heavens! who could do justice to my feelings at this moment! Not conquering heroes themselves in the midst of a triumph – Not the tender mother who has just regained her long-lost infant, and presses it to her heart – Not the weary, hungry mariner at the sight of the desired friendly port – Not the lover, when he once more embraces his beloved mistress after she had been ravished from his arms! – All within my breast was tumult, wildness, and delirium! My feet scarcely touched the ground, for they were winged with joy, and like Elijah, as he rose to Heaven, they 'were with lightning sped as I went on'. Everyone I met I told of my happiness and blazed about the virtue of my amiable master and captain.

When I got to the office and acquainted the Register with my errand he congratulated me on the occasion and told me he would draw up my manumission for half price, which was a guinea. I thanked him for his kindness, and having received it and paid him I hastened to my master to get him to sign it, that I might be fully released. Accordingly he signed the manumission that day, so that before night, I who had been a slave in the morning, trembling at the will of another, was become my own master and completely free. I thought this was the happiest day I had ever experienced; and my joy was still heightened by the blessings and prayers of the sable race, particularly the aged, to whom my heart had ever been attached with reverence.

In short, the fair as well as black people immediately styled me by a new appellation, to me the most desirable in the world, which was Freeman, and at the dances I gave my Georgia superfine blue clothes made no indifferent appearance, as I thought. Some of the sable females who formerly stood aloof now began to relax and appear less coy, but my heart was still fixed on London, where I hoped to be ere long. So that my worthy captain and his owner, my late master, finding that the bent of my mind was towards London, said to me, 'We hope you won't leave us, but that you will still be with the vessels.' Here gratitude bowed me down, and none but the generous mind can judge of my feelings, struggling between inclination and duty. However, notwithstanding my wish to be in London. I obediently answered my benefactors that I could go in the vessel and not leave them, and from that day I was entered on board as an able-bodied sailor at thirty-six shillings per month, besides what perquisites I could make. My intention was to make a voyage or two entirely to please these my honoured patrons, but I determined that the year following, if it pleased God I would see Old England once more and surprise my old master, Capt. Pascal, who was hourly in my mind; for I still loved him, notwithstanding his usage of me, and I pleased myself with thinking of what he would say when he saw what the Lord had done for me in so short a time, instead of being, as he might perhaps suppose, under the cruel yoke of some planter. With these kind of reveries I used often to entertain myself and shorten the time till my return, and now, being as in my original free African state, I embarked on board the *Nancy* after having got all things ready for our voyage. In this state of serenity we sailed for St Eustatia, and having smooth seas and calm weather we soon arrived there: after taking our cargo on board we proceeded to Savannah in Georgia, in August, 1766.

While we were there, as usual, I used to go for the cargo up the rivers in boats, and on this business I have been frequently beset by alligators, which were very numerous on that coast, and I have shot many of them when they have been near getting into our boats; which we have with great difficulty sometimes prevented, and have been very much frightened at them. I have seen a young one sold in Georgia alive for six pence. During our stay at this place, one evening a slave belonging to Mr Read, a merchant of Savannah, came near our vessel, and began to use me very ill. I entreated him, with all the patience I was master of, to desist, as I knew there was little or no law for a free negro here; but the fellow, instead of taking my advice, persevered in his insults, and even struck me. At this I lost all temper, and I fell on him and beat him soundly. The next morning his master came to our vessel as we lay alongside the wharf, and desired me to come ashore that he might have me flogged all round the town, for beating his negro slave. I told him he had insulted me, and had given the provocation, by first striking me. I had told my captain also the whole affair that morning, and wished him to have gone along with me to Mr Read to prevent bad consequences; but he said that it did not signify, and if Mr Read said anything he would make matters up, and had desired me to go to work which I accordingly did. The captain being on board when Mr Read came, he told him I was a free man; and when Mr Read applied to him to deliver me up, he said he knew nothing of the matter. I was astonished and frightened at this, and thought I had better keep where I was than go ashore and be flogged round the town, without judge or jury. I therefore refused to stir; and Mr Read went away, swearing he would bring all the constables in the town, for he would have me out of the vessel. When he was gone, I thought his threat might prove too true to my sorrow; and I was confirmed in this belief, as well by the many instances I had seen of the treatment of free negroes, as from a fact that had happened within my own knowledge here a short time before. There was a free black man, a carpenter, that I knew, who, for asking a gentleman that he worked for for the money he had earned, was put into gaol; and afterwards this oppressed man was sent from Georgia, with false accusations, of an intention to set the gentleman's house on fire, and run away with his slaves. I was therefore much embarrassed, and very apprehensive of a flogging at least. I dreaded, of all things, the thoughts of being striped, as I never in my life had the

marks of any violence of that kind. At that instant a rage
seized my soul, and for a little I determined to resist the
first man that should offer to lay violent hands on me, or
basely use me without a trial; for I would sooner die like
a free man, than suffer myself to be scourged by the hands
of ruffians, and my blood drawn like a slave. The captain
and others, more cautious, advised me to make haste
and conceal myself; for they said Mr Read was a very
spiteful man, and he would soon come on board with
constables and take me. At first I refused this counsel, being
determined to stand my ground; but at length, by the
prevailing entreaties of the captain and Mr Dixon, with
whom he lodged, I went to Mr Dixon's house, which was a
little out of town, at a place called Yea-ma-chra. I was
but just gone when Mr Read, with the constables, came for
me, and searched the vessel; but, not finding me there, he
swore he would have me dead or alive. I was secreted about
five days; however, the good character which my captain
always gave me as well as some other gentlemen who also
knew me, procured me some friends. At last some of
them told my captain that he did not use me well, in
suffering me thus to be imposed upon, and said they would
see me redressed, and get me on board some other vessel.
My captain, on this, immediately went to Mr Read, and
told him, that ever since I eloped from the vessel his work
had been neglected, and he could not go on with her
loading, himself and mate not being well; and, as I had
managed things on board for them, my absence must
retard his voyage, and consequently hurt the owner; he
therefore begged of him to forgive me, as he said he never
had any complaint of me before, for the many years that
I had been with him. After repeated entreaties, Mr Read
said I might go to hell, and that he would not meddle with
me; on which my captain came immediately to me at his
lodging, and, telling me how pleasantly matters had gone

on, he desired me to go on board. Some of my other friends then asked him if he had got the constable's warrant from them; the captain said, No. On this I was desired by them to stay in the house; and they said they would get me on board of some other vessel before the evening. When the captain heard this he became almost distracted. He went immediately for the warrant, and, after using every exertion in his power, he at last got it from my hunters; but I had all the expenses to pay. After I had thanked all my friends for their attention, I went on board again to my work, of which I had always plenty. We were in haste to complete our lading, and were to carry twenty head of cattle with us to the West Indies, where they are a very profitable article.

In order to encourage me in working and to make up for the time I had lost, my captain promised me the privilege of carrying two bullocks of my own with me, and this made me work with redoubled ardour. As soon as I had got the vessel loaded, in doing which I was obliged to perform the duty of the mate as well as my own work, and that the bullocks were coming on board, I asked the captain leave to bring my two, according to his promise; but to my great surprise he told me there was no room for them. I then asked him to permit me to take one, but he said he could not. I was a good deal mortified at this usage, and told him I had no notion that he intended thus to impose on me, nor could I think well of any man that was so much worse than his word. On this we had some disagreement, and I gave him to understand that I intended to leave the vessel. At this he appeared to be very much dejected, and our mate, who had been very sickly and whose duty had long devolved upon me, advised him to persuade me to stay, in consequence of which he spoke very kindly to me, making many fair promises, telling me that, as the mate was so sickly, he could not do without me, and that as the safety of the

vessel and cargo depended greatly upon me he therefore
hoped that I would not be offended at what had passed
between us, and swore he would make up all matters when
we arrived in the West Indies; so I consented to slave on as
before. Soon after this, as the bullocks were coming on
board one of them ran at the captain and butted him so
furiously in the breast, that he never recovered of the
blow. In order to make me some amends for his treatment
about the bullocks, the captain now pressed me very much
to take some turkeys and other fowls with me, and gave me
liberty to take as many as I could find room for, but I
told him he knew very well I had never carried any turkeys
before, as I always thought they were such tender birds
that they were not fit to cross the seas. However he continued to press me to buy them for once, and what was very
surprising to me, the more I was against it, the more he
urged my taking them, insomuch that he insured me from
all losses that might happen by them and I was prevailed
on to take them; but I thought this very strange, as he had
never acted so with me before. This, and not being able to
dispose of my paper-money in any other way, induced me
at length to take four dozen. The turkeys, however, I was
so dissatisfied about that I determined to make no more
voyages to this quarter, nor with this captain, and was very
apprehensive that my free voyage would be the worst I had
ever made. We set sail for Montserrat. The captain and mate
had been both complaining of sickness when we sailed, and
as we proceeded on our voyage they grew worse. This was
about November, and we had not been long at sea before
we began to meet with strong northerly gales and rough
seas, and in about seven or eight days all the bullocks were
near being drowned, and four or five of them died. Our
vessel, which had not been tight at first, was much less so
now, and though we were but nine in the whole, including
five sailors and myself, yet we were obliged to attend to the

pumps every half or three-quarters of an hour. The captain and mate came on deck as often as they were able, which was now but seldom, for they declined so fast that they were not well enough to make observations above four or five times the whole voyage. The whole care of the vessel rested therefore upon me, and I was obliged to direct her by my former experience, not being able to work a traverse. The captain was now very sorry he had not taught me navigation, and protested if ever he should get well again he would not fail to do so, but in about seventeen days his illness increased so much that he was obliged to keep his bed, continuing sensible however till the last, constantly having the owner's interest at heart, for this just and benevolent man ever appeared much concerned about the welfare of what he was entrusted with. When this dear friend found the symptoms of death approaching, he called me by my name, and when I came to him he asked (with almost his last breath) if he had ever done me any harm? 'God forbid I should think so,' I replied, 'I should then be the most ungrateful of wretches to the best of benefactors.' While I was thus expressing my affection and sorrow by his bedside, he expired without saying another word, and the day following we committed his body to the deep. Every man on board loved this man and regretted his death, but I was exceedingly affected at it, and I found that I did not know till he was gone the strength of my regard for him. Indeed I had every reason in the world to be attached to him, for besides that he was in general mild, affable, generous, faithful, benevolent, and just, he was to me a friend and a father, and had it pleased Providence that he had died but five months before, I verily believe I should not have obtained my freedom when I did, and it is not improbable that I might not have been able to get it at any rate afterwards. The captain being dead, the mate came on deck and made such observations as he was able, but to no purpose. In the course of a few days more the few bullocks that remained were found dead, but the turkeys I had, though on the deck and exposed to so much wet and bad weather, did well, and I afterwards gained near 300 per cent on the sale of them, so that in the event it proved a happy circumstance for me that I had not bought the bullocks I intended, for they must have perished with the rest; and I could not help looking on this otherwise trifling circumstance as a particular providence of God, and I was thankful accordingly. The care of the vessel took up all my time, and engaged my attention entirely. As we were now out of the variable winds. I thought I should not be much puzzled to hit upon the islands. I was persuaded I steered right for Antigua, which I wished to reach, as the nearest to us, and in the course of nine or ten days we made this island to our great joy, and the next day after we came to Montserrat. Many were surprised when they heard of my conducting the sloop into the port, and I now obtained a new appellation and was called Captain. This elated me not a little, and it was quite flattering to my vanity to be thus styled by as high a title as any free man in this place possessed. When the death of the captain became known he was much regretted by all who knew him, for he was a man universally respected. At the same time the sable captain lost no fame, for the success I had met with increased the affection of my friends in no small measure.

CHAPTER TEN

Shipwreck in the Bahamas

As I had now, by the death of my captain, lost my great benefactor and friend, I had little inducement to remain longer in the West Indies, except my gratitude to Mr King, which I thought I had pretty well discharged in bringing back his vessel safe and delivering his cargo to his satisfaction. I began to think of leaving this part of the world, of which I had long tired, and returning to England where my heart had always been, but Mr King still pressed me very much to stay with his vessel, and he had done so much for me that I found myself unable to refuse his requests, and consented to go another voyage to Georgia, as the mate, from his ill state of health, was quite useless in the vessel. Accordingly a new captain was appointed whose name was William Phillips, an old acquaintance of mine, and having refitted our vessel and taken several slaves on board, we set sail for St Eustatia, where we stayed by a few days, and on 30 January 1767 we steered for Georgia. Our new captain boasted strangely of his skill in navigating and conducting a vessel, and in consequence of this he steered a new course, several points more to the westward than we ever did before. This appeared to me very extraordinary.

On 4 February, which was soon after we had got into our new course, I dreamt the ship was wrecked amidst the surfs and rocks and that I was the means of saving everyone on board, and on the night following I dreamed the very same dream. These dreams however made no impression on my mind, and the next evening, it being my watch below, I was pumping the vessel a little after eight o'clock just before I went off the deck as is the custom, and being weary with the duty of the day and tired at the pump (for we made a good deal of water) I began to express my impatience, and I uttered with an oath, 'Damn the vessel's bottom out.' But my conscience instantly smote me for the expression. When I left the deck I went to bed and had scarcely fallen asleep when I dreamed the same dream again about the ship that I had dreamt the two preceding nights. At twelve o'clock the watch was changed, and as I had always the charge of the captain's watch, I then went upon deck. At half after one in the morning the man at the helm saw something under the lee-beam that the sea washed against, and he immediately called to me that there was a grampus and desired me to look at it. Accordingly I stood up and observed it for some time, but when I saw the sea wash up against it again and again, I said it was not a fish but a rock. Being soon certain of this, I went down to the captain, and with some confusion told him the danger we were in and desired him to come upon deck immediately. He said it was very well, and I went up again. As soon as I was upon the deck the wind which had been pretty high having abated a little, the vessel began to be carried sideways towards the rock by means of the current. Still the captain did not appear. I therefore went to him again and told him the vessel was then near a large rock, and desired he would come up with speed. He said he would and I returned to the deck. When I was upon the deck again I saw we were not above a pistol shot from the rock, and I heard the noise of the breakers all around us. I was exceedingly alarmed at this, and the captain having not yet come on the deck I lost all patience, and growing quite enraged, I ran down to him again and asked him why he did not come up and what he could mean by all this? 'The breakers,' said I, 'are round us, and the vessel is almost on the rock.' With that he came on the deck with me, and we tried to put the vessel about and get her out of the current, but all to no purpose, the wind being very small. We then called all hands up immediately, and after a little we got up one end of a cable and fastened it to the anchor. By this time the surf was foaming round us and made a dreadful noise on the breakers, and the very moment we let the anchor go the vessel struck against the rocks. One swell now succeeded another, as it were one wave calling on its fellow: the roaring of the billows increased, and with one single heave of the swells the sloop was pierced and transfixed among the rocks! In a moment a scene of horror presented itself to my mind such as I never had conceived or experienced before. All my sins stared me in the face, and especially I thought that God had hurled his direful vengeance on my guilty head for cursing the vessel on which my life depended. My spirits at this forsook me and I expected every moment to go to the bottom: I determined if I should still be saved that I would never swear again. And in the midst of my distress, while the dreadful surfs were dashing with unremitting fury among the rocks, I remembered the Lord, though fearful that I was undeserving of forgiveness, and I thought that as he had often delivered he might yet deliver, and calling to mind the many mercies he had shown me in times past, they gave me some small hope that he might still help me. I then began to think how we might be saved, and I believe no mind was ever like mine so replete with inventions and confused with schemes, though how to escape death I knew not. The captain immediately ordered the hatches to be nailed down on the slaves in the hold, where there were above twenty, all of whom must unavoidably have perished if he had been obeyed. When he desired the man to nail down the hatches I thought that my sin was the cause of this and that God would charge me with these people's blood. This thought rushed upon my mind that instant with such violence that it quite overpowered me, and I fainted. I recovered just as the people were about to nail down the hatches, perceiving which, I desired them to stop. The captain then said it must be done: I asked him why? He said that everyone would endeavour to get into the boat, which was but small, and thereby we should be drowned, for it would not have carried above ten at the most. I could no longer restrain my emotion, and I told him he deserved drowning for not knowing how to navigate the vessel; and I believe the people would have tossed him overboard if I had given them the least hint of it. However the hatches were not nailed down, and as none of us could leave the vessel then on account of the darkness, and as we knew not where to go and were convinced besides that the boat could not survive the surfs, we all said we would remain on the dry part of the vessel and trust to God till daylight appeared, when we should know better what to do.

I then advised to get the boat prepared against morning and some of us began to set about it, but some abandoned all care of the ship and themselves and fell to drinking. Our boat had a piece out of her bottom near two feet long and we had no materials to mend her. However, necessity being the mother of invention, I took some pump leather and nailed it to the broken part and plastered it over with tallow-grease. And thus prepared, with the utmost anxiety of mind we watched for daylight, and thought every minute an hour till it appeared. At last it saluted our longing eyes, and kind Providence accompanied its approach with what was no small comfort to us, for the dreadful swell began to subside, and the next thing that we discovered to raise our dropping spirits was a small key or island about five or six miles off. But a barrier soon presented itself, for there was not water enough for our boat to go over the reefs and this threw us again into a sad consternation. But there was no alternative, we were therefore obliged to put but few in the boat at once, and what is still worse, all of us were frequently under the necessity of getting out to drag and lift it over the reefs. This cost us much labour and fatigue, and what was yet more distressing, we could not avoid having our legs cut and torn very much with the rocks. There were only four people that would work with me at the oars, and they consisted of three black men and a Dutch creole sailor; and though we went with the boat five times that day we had no others to assist us. But had we not worked in this manner I really believe the people could not have been saved, for not one of the white men did anything to preserve their lives, and indeed they soon got so drunk that they were not able, but lay about the deck like swine, so that we were at last obliged to lift them into the boat and carry them on shore by force. This want of assistance made our labour intolerably severe, insomuch that by putting on shore so often that day, the skin was entirely stripped off my hands.

However we continued all the day to toil and strain our exertions till we had brought all on board safe to the shore, so that out of thirty-two people we lost not one. My dream now returned upon my mind with all its force; it was fulfilled in every part, for our danger was the same I had dreamt of; and I could not help looking on myself as the principal instrument in effecting our deliverance, for owing to some of our people getting drunk the rest of us were obliged to double our exertions, and it was fortunate we did, for in a very little time longer the patch of leather on the boat would have been worn out and she would have been no longer fit for service. Situated as we were, who could think that men should be so careless of the danger they

were in? For if the wind had but raised the swell as it was
when the vessel struck we must have bid a final farewell to
all hopes of deliverance; and though I warned the people
who were drinking and entreated them to embrace the
moment of deliverance, nevertheless they persisted, as if not
possessed of the least spark of reason. I could not help
thinking, that if any of these people had been lost God
would charge me with their lives, which perhaps was one
cause of my labouring so hard for their preservation, and
indeed every one of them afterwards seemed so sensible of
the service I had rendered them, and while we were on
the key I was a kind of chieftain amongst them. I brought
some limes, oranges, and lemons ashore, and finding it to
be a good soil where we were I planted several of them as a
token to anyone that might be cast away hereafter. This,
key as we afterwards found, was one of the Bahama islands,
which consist of a cluster of large islands with smaller ones
or keys as they are called interspersed among them. It was
about a mile in circumference, with a white sandy beach
running in a regular order along it. On that part of it
where we first attempted to land there stood some very
large birds called flamingos: these, from the reflection of
the sun, appeared to us at a little distance as large as men,
and when they walked backwards and forwards we could
not conceive what they were. Our captain swore they were
cannibals. This created a great panic among us, and we
held a consultation how to act. The captain wanted to go
to a key that was within sight but a great way off, but
I was against it, as in so doing we should not be able to save
all the people. 'And therefore,' said I, 'let us go on shore
here, and perhaps these cannibals may take to the water.'
Accordingly we steered towards them, and when we
approached them, to our very great joy and no less wonder
they walked off one after the other very deliberately, and
at last they took flight and relieved us entirely from our

fears. About the key there were turtles and several sorts of
fish in such abundance that we caught them without bait,
which was a great relief to us after the salt provisions on
board. There was also a large rock on the beach, about ten
feet high, which was in the form of a punch-bowl at the tip.
This we could not help thinking Providence had ordained
to supply us with rainwater, and it was something singular
that if we did not take the water when it rained, in some
little time after it would turn as salt as sea-water.

Our first care after refreshment was to make ourselves
tents to lodge in, which we did as well as we could with
some sails we had brought from the ship. We then began to
think how we might get from this place, which was quite
uninhabited, and we determined to repair our boat, which
was very much shattered, and to put to sea in quest of a
ship or some inhabited island. It took us however eleven
days before we could get the boat ready for sea in the
manner we wanted it, with a sail and other necessaries.
When we had got all things prepared the captain wanted
me to stay on shore while he went to sea in quest of a vessel
to take all the people off the key, but this I refused, and the
captain and myself, with five more, set off in the boat
towards New Providence. We had no more than two
musket load of gunpowder with us if anything should
happen, and our stock of provisions consisted of three
gallons of rum, four of water, some salt beef, and some
biscuit; and in this manner we proceeded to sea.

On the second day of our voyage we came to an island
called Abaco, the largest of the Bahama islands. We were
much in want of water, for by this time our water was
expended and we were exceedingly fatigued in pulling
for two days in the heat of the sun; and it being late in the
evening, we hauled the boat ashore to try for water and
remain during the night. When we came ashore we
searched for water but could find none. When it was dark,

we made a fire around us for fear of the wild beasts, as the
place was an entire thick wood, and we took it by turns to
watch. In this situation we found very little rest and waited
with impatience for the morning. As soon as the light
appeared we set off again with our boat in hopes of finding
assistance during the day. We were now much dejected
and weakened by pulling the boat, for our sail was of no
use, and we were almost famished for want of fresh water
to drink. We had nothing left to eat but salt beef and that
we could not use without water. In this situation we toiled
all day in sight of the island, which was very long. In the
evening, seeing no relief, we made ashore again and
fastened our boat. We then went to look for fresh water,
being quite faint for the want of it, and we dug and
searched about for some all the remainder of the evening
but could not find one drop, so that our dejection at this
period became excessive, and our terror so great that we
expected nothing but death to deliver us. We could not
touch our beef, which was as salt as brine, without fresh
water, and we were in the greatest terror from the apprehension of wild beasts. When unwelcome night came we
acted as on the night before, and the next morning we set
off again from the island in hopes of seeing some vessel.
In this manner we toiled as well as we were able till four
o'clock, during which we passed several keys but could not
meet with a ship, and still famishing with thirst, went
ashore on one of those keys again in hopes of finding some
water. Here we found some leaves with a few drops of
water in them, which we lapped with much eagerness. We
then dug in several places, but without success. As we
were digging holes in search of water there came forth some
very thick and black stuff, but none of us could touch it,
except the poor Dutch Creole, who drank above a quart
of it as eagerly as if it had been wine. We tried to catch fish
but could not, and we now began to repine at our fate and

abandon ourselves to despair, when in the midst of our murmuring, the captain all at once cried out, 'A sail! a sail! a sail!' This gladdening sound was like a reprieve to a convict and we all instantly turned to look at it, but in a little time some of us began to be afraid it was not a sail. However, at a venture, we embarked and steered after it, and in half an hour, to our unspeakable joy we plainly saw that it was a vessel. At this our drooping spirits revived and we made towards her with all the speed imaginable. When we came near to her, we found she was a little sloop about the size of a Gravesend hoy and quite full of people, a circumstance which we could not make the meaning of. Our captain, who was a Welshman, swore that they were pirates and would kill us. I said, be that as it might, we must board her if we were to die for it, and if they should not receive us kindly we must oppose them as well as we could, for there was no alternative between their perishing and ours. This counsel was immediately taken, and I really believe that the captain, myself, and the Dutchman would then have faced twenty men. We had two cutlasses and a musket that I brought in the boat, and in this situation we rowed alongside and immediately boarded her. I believe there were about forty hands on board, but how great was our surprise, as soon as we got on board, to find that the major part of them were in the same predicament as ourselves!

They belonged to a whaling schooner that was wrecked two days before us about nine miles to the north of our vessel. When she was wrecked some of them had taken to their boats and had left some of their people and property on a key in the same manner as we had done, and were going, like us, to New Providence in quest of a ship, when they met with this little sloop, called a wrecker, their employment in those seas being to look after wrecks. They were then going to take the remainder of the people belonging to the schooner, for which the wrecker was to have all things belonging to the vessel, and likewise their people's help to get what they could out of her and were then to carry the crew to New Providence.

We told the people of the wrecker the condition of our vessel and we made the same agreement with them as the schooner's people, and on their complying, we begged of them to go to our key directly because our people were in want of water. They agreed, therefore, to go along with us first, and in two days we arrived at the key to the inexpressible joy of the people that we had left behind, as they had been reduced to great extremities for want of water in our absence. Luckily for us, the wrecker had now more people on board than she could carry or victual for any moderate length of time. They therefore hired the schooner's people to work on our wreck, and we left them our boat and embarked for New Providence.

We stayed in New Providence about seventeen or eighteen days, during which time I met with many friends, who gave me encouragement to stay there with them. But I declined it, though had not my heart been fixed on England I should have stayed, as I liked the place extremely, and there were some free black people here who were very happy, and we passed our time pleasantly together with the melodious sound of the catguts, under the lime and lemon trees. At length Captain Phillips hired a sloop to carry him and some of the slaves that he could not sell to Georgia, and I agreed to go with him in this vessel, meaning now to take my farewell of that place. When the vessel was ready we all embarked, and I took leave of New Providence, not without regret. We sailed about four o'clock in the morning with a fair wind for Georgia, and about eleven o'clock the same morning a short and sudden gale sprung up and blew away most of our sails, and as we were still amongst the keys, in a very few minutes it dashed the sloop against the rocks. Luckily for us the water was deep and the sea was not so angry but that, after having for some time laboured hard, and being many in number, we were saved through God's mercy; and by using our greatest exertions we got the vessel off. The next day we returned to Providence, where we soon got her again refitted. Some of the people swore that we had spells set upon us by somebody in Montserrat, and others that we had witches and wizards amongst the poor helpless slaves, and that we never should arrive safe at Georgia. But these things did not deter me. I said, 'Let us again face the winds and seas, and swear not, but trust to God, and he will deliver us.' We therefore once more set sail, and with hard labour in seven days' time arrived safe at Georgia.

After our arrival we went up to the town of Savannah, and the same evening I went to a friend's house to lodge, whose name was Mosa, a black man. We were very happy at meeting each other, and after supper we had a light till it was between nine and ten o'clock at night. About that time the watch or patrol came by, and discerning a light in the house they knocked at the door: we opened it, and they came in and sat down and drank some punch with us. They also begged some limes of me, as they understood I had some, which I readily gave them. A little after this they told me I must go to the watch-house with them. This surprised me a good deal after our kindness to them, and I asked them, Why so? They said that all negroes who had light in their houses after nine o'clock were to be taken into custody and either pay some dollars or be flogged. Some of those people knew that I was a free man, but as the man of the house was not free and had his master to protect him, they did not take the same liberty with him they did with me. I told them that I was a free man and just arrived from Providence, that we were not making any noise and that I was not a stranger in that place, but was very well known there. 'Besides,' said I, 'what will you do with me?' – 'That you shall see,' replied they, 'but you must go to the watch-house with us,' Now whether they meant to get money from me or not I was at a loss to know, but I thought immediately of the oranges and limes at Santa Cruz, and seeing that nothing would pacify them I went with them to the watch-house, where I remained during the night. Early the next morning these imposing ruffians flogged a negro-man and woman that they had in the watch-house and then they told me that I must be flogged too. I asked why? and if there was no law for free men? And told them if there was I would have it put in force against them. But this only exasperated them the more, and instantly they swore they would serve me as Doctor Perkins had done. And they were going to lay violent hands on me, when one of them, more humane than the rest, said that as I was a free man they could not justify stripping me by law. I then immediately sent for Doctor Brady, who was known to be an honest and worthy man, and on his coming to my assistance they let me go. This was not the only disagreeable incident I met with while I was in this place, for one day while I was a little way out of the town of Savannah, I was beset by two white men who meant to play their usual tricks with me in the way of kidnapping. As soon as these men accosted me, one of them said to the other, 'This is the very fellow we are looking for that you lost:' and the other swore immediately that I was the identical person. On this they made up to me and were about to handle me, but I told them to be still and keep off, for I had seen those kind of tricks played upon other free blacks and they must not think to serve me so. At this they paused a little, and one said to the other –'It will not do;' and the other answered that I talked too good

English. I replied, I believed I did, and I had also with me a revengeful stick equal to the occasion, and my mind was likewise good. Happily however it was not used, and after we had talked together a little in this manner the rogues left me. I stayed in Savannah for some time, anxiously trying to get to Montserrat once more to see Mr King, my old master, and then to take a final farewell of the American quarter of the globe. At last I met with a sloop called the *Speedwell*. Captain John Bunton, which belonged to Grenada and was bound to Martinique, a French island, with a cargo of rice, and I shipped myself on board of her. Before I left Georgia a black woman, who had a child lying dead, being very tenacious of the church burial service and not able to get any white person to perform it, applied to me for that purpose. I told her I was no parson, and besides, that the service over the dead did not affect the soul. This however did not satisfy her, she still urged me very hard. I therefore complied with her earnest entreaties, and at last consented to act the parson for the first time in my life. As she was much respected, there was a great company both of white and black people at the grave. I then accordingly assumed my new vocation, and performed the funeral ceremony to the satisfaction of all present, after which I bade adieu to Georgia, and sailed for Martinique.

CHAPTER ELEVEN

Return to Europe

I THUS took a final leave of Georgia, for the treatment I had received in it disgusted me very much against the place, and when I left it and sailed for Martinique I determined never more to revisit it. My new captain conducted his vessel safer than my former one, and after an agreeable voyage we got safe to our intended port. While I was on this island I went about a good deal and found it pleasant. In particular I admired the town of St Pierre, which is the principal one in the island, and built more like an European town than any I had seen in the West Indies. In general also, slaves were better treated, had more holidays, and looked better than those in the English islands. After we had done our business here I wanted my discharge, which was necessary, for it was then the month of May and I wished much to be at Montserrat to bid farewell to Mr King and all my other friends there in time to sail to England in the July fleet. But, alas! I had put a great stumbling block in my own way by which I was near losing my passage that season to England. I had lent my captain some money, which I now wanted to enable me to prosecute my intentions. This I told him, but when I applied for it, though I urged the necessity of my occasion, I met with so much shuffling from him that I began at last to be afraid of losing my money as I could not recover it by law: for I have already mentioned that throughout the West Indies no black man's testimony is admitted, on any occasion, against any white person whatever, and therefore my own oath would have been of no use.

At last, however, with a great many entreaties I got my money from the captain, and took the first vessel I could meet with for St Eustatia. From thence I went in another to Basseterre in St Kitts, where I arrived on 19 July. On the 22nd, having met with a vessel bound for Montserrat, I wanted to go in her, but the captain and others would not take me on board until I should advertise myself and give notice of my going off the island. I told them of my haste to be in Montserrat and that the time then would not admit of advertising, it being late in the evening and the captain about to sail. But he insisted it was necessary, and otherwise he said he would not take me. This reduced me to great perplexity, for if I should be compelled to submit to this degrading necessity which every black freeman is under, of advertising himself like a slave when he leaves an island, and which I thought a gross imposition upon any freeman, I feared I should miss that opportunity of going to Montserrat, and then I could not get to England that year. The vessel was just going off and no time could be lost. I immediately therefore set about with a heavy heart to try who I could get to befriend me in complying with the demands of the captain. Luckily I found in a few minutes some gentleman of Montserrat whom I knew and, having told him my situation I requested their friendly assistance in helping me off the island. Some of them on this went with me to the captain and satisfied him of my freedom, and to my very great joy he desired me to go on board. We then set sail and the next day, the 23rd, I arrived at the wished-for place after an absence of six months in which I had more than once experienced the delivering hand of

Providence when all human means of escaping destruction seemed hopeless. I saw my friends with a gladness of heart which was increased by my absence and the dangers I had escaped, and I was received with great friendship by them all, but particularly by Mr King, to whom I related the fate of his sloop, the *Nancy*, and the causes of her being wrecked. I now learned with extreme sorrow that his house was washed away during my absence by the bursting of a pond at the top of a mountain that was opposite the town of Plymouth. It swept great parts of the town away and Mr King lost a great deal of property from the inundation and nearly his life. When I told him I intended to go to London that season and that I had come to visit him before my departure, the good man expressed a great deal of affection for me and sorrow that I should leave him, and warmly advised me to stay there, insisting, as I was much respected by all the gentlemen in the place, that I might do very well, and in a short time have land and slaves of my own. I thanked him for this instance of his friendship, but as I wished very much to be in London, I declined remaining any longer there and begged he would excuse me. I then requested he would be kind enough to give me a certificate of my behaviour while in his service, which he very readily complied with, and gave me the following:

Montserrat, January 26, 1767

The bearer hereof, Gustavus Vassa, was my slave for upwards of three years, during which he has always behaved himself well, and discharged his duty with honesty and assiduity.

ROBERT KING

To all whom this may concern.

Having obtained this, I parted from my kind master after many sincere professions of gratitude and regard,

and prepared for my departure for London. I immediately
agreed to go with one Capt. John Hamer, for seven
guineas the passage to London, on board a ship called the
Andromache, and on the 24th and 25th I had free dances,
as they are called, with some of my countrymen, previous
to my setting off, after which I took leave of all my friends
and on the 26th I embarked for London, exceedingly glad
to see myself once more on board of a ship, and still more so
in steering the course I had long wished for. With a light
heart I bade Montserrat farewell and never had my feet
on it since; and with it I bade adieu to the sound of the
cruel whip and all other dreadful instruments of torture;
adieu to the offensive sight of the violated chastity of the
sable females, which has too often accosted my eyes;
adieu to oppressions (although to me less severe than most
of my countrymen); and adieu to the angry howling,
dashing surfs. I wished for a grateful and thankful heart
to praise the Lord God on high for all his mercies!

We had a most prosperous voyage, and at the end of
seven weeks arrived at Cherry Garden Stairs. Thus
were my longing eyes once more gratified with a sight of
London after having been absent from it above four years.
I immediately received my wages, and I never had earned
seven guineas so quick in my life before. I had thirty-seven
guineas in all, when I got cleared of the ship. I now entered
upon a scene quite new to me but full of hope. In this
situation my first thoughts were to look out for some of my
former friends, and amongst the first of those were the Miss
Guerins. As soon therefore as I had regaled myself I went in
quest of those kind ladies, whom I was very impatient to
see, and with some difficulty and perseverance, I found
them at May's-hill, Greenwich. They were most agreeably
surprised to see me, and I quite overjoyed at meeting
with them. I told them my history, at which they expressed
great wonder and freely acknowledged it did their cousin,

Capt. Pascal, no honour. He then visited there frequently,
and I met him four or five days after in Greenwich Park.
When he saw me he appeared a good deal surprised and
asked me how I came back? I answered, 'In a ship.' To
which he replied dryly, 'I suppose you did not walk back
to London on the water.' As I saw by his manner that he
did not seem to be sorry for his behaviour to me, and that
I had not much reason to expect any favour from him, I
told him that he had used me very ill after I had been such
a faithful servant to him for so many years, on which,
without saying any more, he turned about and went away.
A few days after this I met Capt. Pascal at Miss Guerin's
house, and asked him for my prize-money. He said there
was none due to me, for if my prize-money had been
£10,000 he had a right to it all. I told him I was informed
otherwise, on which he bade me defiance and, in a banter-
ing tone, desired me to commence a law-suit against him
for it: 'There are lawyers enough,' said he, 'that will take
the case in hand, and you had better try it.' I told him
then that I would try it, which enraged him very much;
however, out of regard to the ladies I remained still and
never made any further demand of my right. Some time
afterwards these friendly ladies asked me what I meant to
do with myself and how they could assist me. I thanked
them and said if they pleased I would be their servant, but
if not, as I had thirty-seven guineas which would support
me for some time, I would be much obliged to them to
recommend me to some person who would teach me a
business whereby I might earn my living. They answered
me very politely that they were sorry it did not suit them
to take me as their servant, and asked me what business I
should like to learn? I said hairdressing. They then
promised to assist me in this, and soon after they recommended me to a gentleman whom I had known before,
one Capt. O'Hara, who treated me with much kindness

and procured me a master, a hairdresser, in Coventry-Court, Haymarket, with whom he placed me. I was with this man from September till the February following. In that time we had a neighbour in the same court who taught the French horn. He used to blow it so well that I was charmed with it and agreed with him to teach me to blow it. Accordingly he took me in hand and began to instruct me, and I soon learned all the three parts. I took great delight in blowing on this instrument, the evening being long, and besides that I was fond of it, I did not like to be idle and it filled up my vacant hours innocently. At this time also I agreed with the Rev. Mr Gregory, who lived in the same court where he kept an academy and an evening school, to improve me in arithmetic. This he did as far as barter and alligation, so that all the time I was there I was entirely employed. In February 1768 I hired myself to Dr Charles Irving, in Pall-mall, so celebrated for his successful experiments in making sea-water fresh, and here I had plenty of hairdressing to improve my hand. This gentleman was an excellent master. He was exceedingly kind and good tempered, and allowed me in the evenings to attend my schools, which I esteemed a great blessing. Therefore I thanked God and him for it and used all my diligence to improve the opportunity. This diligence and attention recommended me to the notice and care of my three preceptors, who on their parts bestowed a great deal of pains in my instruction, and besides were all very kind to me. My wages, however, which by two-thirds less than I ever had in my life (for I had only £12 per annum) I soon found would not be sufficient to defray this extra-ordinary expense of masters and my own necessary expenses. My old thirty-seven guineas had by this time worn all away to one. I thought it best therefore to try the sea again in quest of more money, as I had been bred to it, and had hitherto found the profession of it successful.

I had also a very great desire to see Turkey and I now determined to gratify it. Accordingly, in the month of May 1768, I told the doctor my wish to go to sea again, to which he made no opposition, and we parted on friendly terms. The same day I went into the city in quest of a master. I was extremely fortunate in my inquiry, for I soon heard of a gentleman who had a ship going to Italy and Turkey, and he wanted a man who could dress hair well. I was overjoyed at this and went immediately on board of his ship as I had been directed, which I found to be fitted up with great taste, and I already foreboded no small pleasure in sailing in her. Not finding the gentleman on board I was directed to his lodgings, where I met with him the next day and gave him a specimen of my dressing. He liked t so well that he hired me immediately, so that I was perfectly happy, for the ship, master, and voyage, were entirely to my mind. The ship was called the *Delaware*, and my master's name was John Jolly, a neat smart good-humoured man, just such as one as I wished to serve. We sailed from England in July following and our voyage was extremely pleasant. We went to Villa Franca, Nice, and Leghorn, and in all these place I was charmed with the richness and beauty of the countries and struck with the elegant buildings with which they abound. We had always in them plenty of extraordinary good wines and rich fruits, which I was very fond of. When we left Italy we had delightful sailing among the Archipelago islands, and from thence to Smyrna, in Turkey. This is a very ancient city. The houses are built of stone, and most of them have graves adjoining to them, so that they sometimes present the appearance of churchyards. Provisions are very plentiful in this city and good wine less than a penny a pint. The grapes, pomegranates and many other fruits were also the richest and largest I ever tasted. The natives are well looking and strong made, and treated me always

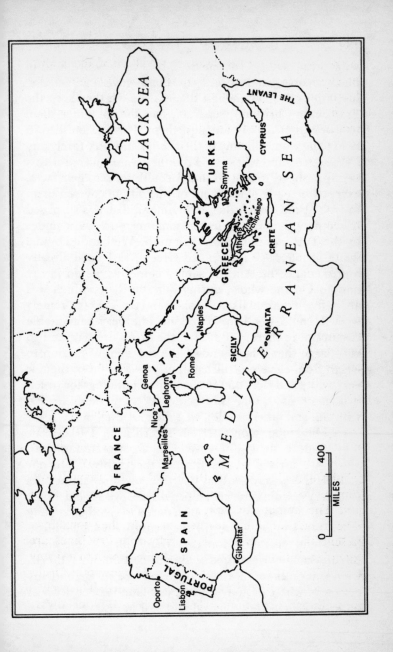

with great civility. In general I believe they are fond of
black people, and several of them gave me pressing
invitations to stay amongst them, although they keep the
Franks, or Christians, separate, and do not suffer them
to dwell immediately amongst them. I was astonished in
not seeing women in any of their shops and very rarely any
in the street, and whenever I did they were covered with a
veil from head to foot so that I could not see their faces,
except when any of them out of curiosity uncovered them
to look at me, which they sometimes did. I was surprised
to see how the Greeks are, in some measure, kept under
by the Turks, as the negroes are in the West Indies by the
white people. The less refined Greeks, as I have already
hinted, dance here in the same manner as we do in my
nation. On the whole, during our stay here, which was
about five months. I liked the place and the Turks extremely
well. I could not help observing one very remarkable
circumstance there: the tails of the sheep are flat, and so
very large that I have known the tail even of a lamb to
weigh from eleven to thirteen pounds. The fat of them is
very white and rich, and is excellent in puddings for which
it is much used. Our ship being at length richly loaded
with silk and other articles, we sailed for England.

In May 1769, soon after our return from Turkey, our
ship made a delightful voyage to Oporto in Portugal,
where we arrived at the time of the carnival. On our
arrival, there were sent on board to us thirty-six articles
to observe, with very heavy penalties if we should break
any of them, and none of us even dared to go on board any
other vessel or on shore till the Inquisition had sent on
board and searched for everything illegal, especially
Bibles. Such as were produced, and certain other things,
were sent on shore till the ships were going away, and any
person in whose custody a Bible was found concealed was
to be imprisoned and flogged and sent into slavery for ten

years. I saw here many very magnificent sights, particularly the Garden of Eden, where many of the clergy and laity went in procession in their several orders with the host, and sung Te Deum. I had a great curiosity to go into some of their churches, but could not gain admittance without using the necessary sprinkling of holy water at my entrance. From curiosity, and a wish to be holy, I therefore complied with this ceremony, but its virtues were lost on me for I found myself nothing the better for it. This place abounds with plenty of all kinds of provisions. The town is well built and pretty, and commands a fine prospect. Our ship having taken in a load of wine and other commodities, we sailed for London, and arrived in July following. Our next voyage was to the Mediterranean. The ship was again got ready and we sailed in September for Genoa. This is one of the finest cities I ever saw. Some of the edifices were of beautiful marble and made a most noble appearance, and many had very curious fountains before them. The churches were rich and magnificent and curiously adorned both in the inside and out. But all this grandeur was in my eyes disgraced by the galley slaves, whose condition both there and in other parts of Italy is truly piteous and wretched. After we had stayed there some weeks, during which we bought many different things which we wanted and got them very cheap, we sailed to Naples, a charming city and remarkably clean. The bay is the most beautiful I ever saw; the moles for shipping are excellent. I thought it extraordinary to see grand operas acted here on Sunday nights, and even attended by their majesties. I too, like these great ones, went to those sights, and vainly served God in the day while I thus served mammon effectually at night. While we remained here there happened an eruption of Mount Vesuvius, of which I had a perfect view. It was extremely awful, and we were so near that the ashes from it used to be thick on our deck. After we had transacted our business at Naples we sailed with a fair wind once more for Smyrna, where we arrived in December. A seraskier or officer took a liking to me here, and wanted me to stay, and offered me two wives. However I refused the temptation. The merchants here travel in caravans or large companies. I have seen many caravans from India with some hundreds of camels laden with different goods. The people of these caravans are quite brown. Among other articles, they brought with them a great quantity of locusts, which are a kind of pulse, sweet and pleasant to the palate, and in shape resembling French beans but longer. Each kind of goods is sold in a street by itself and I always found the Turks very honest in their dealings. They let no Christians into their mosques or churches, for which I was very sorry, as I was always fond of going to see the different modes of worship of the people wherever I went. The plague broke out while we were in Smyrna, and we stopped taking goods into the ship till it was over. She was then richly laden, and we sailed in about March 1770 for England.

One day in our passage we met with an accident which was near burning the ship. A black cook, in melting some fat, overset the pan into the fire under the deck, which immediately began to blaze, and the flame went up very high under the foretop. With the fright the poor cook became almost white, and altogether speechless. Happily however we got the fire out without doing much mischief. After various delays in this passage, which was tedious, we arrived in Standgate creek in July; and, at the latter end of the year, some new event occurred, so that my noble captain, the ship, and I all separated.

In April 1771 I shipped myself as a steward with Capt. Wm Robertson of the ship *Grenada Planter*, once more to try my fortune in the West Indies; and we sailed from London for Madeira, Barbados, and the Grenadas. When

we were at this last place, having some goods to sell, I met
once more with my former kind of West India customers. A
white man, an islander, bought some goods from me to the
amount of some pounds, and made me many fair promises
as usual, but without any intention of paying me. He had
likewise bought goods from some more of our people,
whom he intended to serve in the same manner; but he still
amused us with promises. However, when our ship was
loaded, and near sailing, this honest buyer discovered no
intention or sign of paying for anything he had bought of
us; but on the contrary, when I asked him for my money
he threatened me and another black man he had bought
goods of, so that we found we were like to get more blows
than payment. On this we went to complain to one Mr
McIntosh, a justice of the peace; we told his worship of
the man's villainous tricks, and begged that he would be
kind enough to see us redressed: but being negroes, although
free, we could not get any remedy; and our ship being then
just upon the point of sailing, we knew not how to help
ourselves, though we thought it hard to lose our property
in this manner. Luckily for us however, this man was also
indebted to three white sailors, who could not get a farthing
from him; they therefore readily joined us, and we all
went together in search of him. When we found where he
was, I took him out of a house and threatened him with
vengeance; on which, finding he was likely to be handled
roughly, the rogue offered each of us some small allowance,
but nothing near our demands. This exasperated us much
more; and some were for cutting his ears off; but he begged
hard for mercy, which was at last granted him, after we
had entirely stripped him. We then let him go, for which
he thanked us, glad to get off so easily, and ran into the
bushes, after having wished us a good voyage. We then
repaired on board and shortly after set sail for England. I
cannot help remarking here a very narrow escape we had

from being blown up, owing to a piece of negligence of mine. Just as our ship was under sail, I went down into the cabin to do some business, and had a lighted candle in my hand, which, in my hurry, without thinking, I held in a barrel of gunpowder. It remained in the powder until it was near catching fire, when fortunately I observed it and snatched it out in time, and providentially no harm happened; but I was so overcome with terror that I immediately fainted at this deliverance.

In twenty-eight days' time we arrived in England, and I got clear of this ship. But, being still of a roving disposition, and desirous of seeing as many different parts of the world as I could, I shipped myself soon after, in the same year, as steward on board of a fine large ship, called the *Jamaica*, Captain David Watt; and we sailed from England in December 1771 for Nevis and Jamaica. I found Jamaica to be a very fine large island, well peopled, and the most considerable of the West India islands. There was a vast number of negroes here, whom I found as usual exceedingly imposed upon by the white people, and the slaves punished as in the other islands. There are negroes whose business it is to flog slaves; they go about to different people for employment, and the usual pay is from one to four bits. I saw many cruel punishments inflicted on the slaves in the short time I stayed here. In particular I was present when a poor fellow was tied up and kept hanging by the wrists at some distance from the ground, and then some half hundredweights were fixed to his ankles, in which posture he was flogged unmercifully. There were also, as I heard, two different masters noted for cruelty on the island, who had staked up two negroes naked, and in two hours the vermin stung them to death. I heard a gentleman I well knew tell my captain that he passed sentence on a negro man to be burnt alive for attempting to poison an overseer. I pass over numerous other instances, in order to relieve the reader by a milder scene of roguery. Before I had been long on the island, one Mr Smith at Port Morant bought goods of me to the amount of twenty-five pounds sterling; but when I demanded payment from him, he was going each time to beat me, and threatened that he would put me in goal. One time he would say I was going to set his house on fire, at another he would swear I was going to run away with his slaves. I was astonished at this usage from a person who was in the situation of a gentleman, but I had no alternative; I was therefore obliged to submit.

When I came to Kingston I was surprised to see the number of Africans who were assembled together on Sundays, particularly at a large commodious place called Spring Path. Here each different nation of Africa meet and dance after the manner of their own country. They still retain most of their native customs: they bury their dead and put victuals, pipes and tobacco, and other things in the grave with the corpse in the same manner as in Africa. Our ship having got her loading we sailed for London, where we arrived in the August following. On my return to London, I waited on my old and good master, Dr Irving, who made me an offer of his service again. Being now tired of the sea I gladly accepted it. I was very happy in living with this gentleman once more, during which time we were daily employed in reducing old Neptune's dominions by purifying the briny element and making it fresh. Thus I went on till May 1773, when I was roused by the sound of fame to seek new adventures, and to find, towards the North Pole what our Creator never intended we should, a passage to India.

CHAPTER TWELVE

Arctic Exploration

AN expedition was now fitting out to explore a north-east passage, conducted by the Honourable John Constantine Phipps, since Lord Mulgrave, in his Majesty's sloop-of-war the *Race Horse*. My master being anxious for the reputation of this adventure, we therefore prepared everything for our voyage, and I attended him on board the *Race Horse*, 24 May 1773. We proceeded to Sheerness where we were joined by his Majesty's sloop the *Carcass*, commanded by Captain Lutwidge. On 4 June we sailed towards our destined place, the Pole, and on the 15th of the same month we were off Shetland. On this day I had a great and unexpected deliverance from an accident which was near blowing up the ship and destroying the crew, which made me ever after during the voyage uncommonly cautious. The ship was so filled that there was very little room on board for anyone, which placed me in an awkward situation. I had resolved to keep a journal of this singular and interesting voyage, and I had no other place for this purpose but a little cabin, or the doctor's store-room, where I slept. This little place was stuffed with all manner of combustibles, particularly with tow and aquafortis, and many other dangerous things. Unfortunately it happened in the evening as I was writing my journal that I had occasion to take the candle out of the lantern, and a spark having touched a single thread of the tow, all the rest caught flame and immediately the whole was in a blaze. I saw nothing but present death before me and expected to be the first to perish in the flames. In a moment the alarm was spread and many people who were near ran to assist in putting out the fire. All this time I was in the very midst of the flames. My shirt and the handkerchief on my neck were burnt, and I was almost smothered with the smoke. However, through God's mercy, as I was nearly giving up all hopes, some people brought blankets and mattresses and threw them on the flames, by which means in a short time the fire was put out. I was severely reprimanded and menaced by such of the officers who knew it, and strictly charged never more to go there with a light: and indeed, even my own fears made me give heed to this command for a little time, but at last, not being able to write my journal in any other part of the ship, I was tempted again to venture by stealth with a light in the same cabin, though not without considerable fear and dread on my mind. On 20 June we began to use Dr Irving's apparatus for making salt-water fresh. I used to attend the distillery. I frequently purified from twenty-six to forty gallons a day. The water thus distilled was perfectly pure, well tasted, and free from salt, and was used on various occasions on board the ship. On 28 June, being in lat. 78°, we made Greenland, where I was surprised to see the sun did not set. The weather now became extremely cold, and as we sailed between north and east, which was our course, we saw many very high and curious mountains of ice, and also a great number of very large whales which used to come close to our ship and blow the water up to a very great height in the air. One morning we had vast quantities of sea-horses about the ship, which neighed exactly like any other horses. We fired some harpoon guns amongst them in order to take some, but we could not get any. The 30th, the captain of a Greenland ship came on board and told us of three ships that were lost in the ice. However we still held on our course till 11 July, when we were stopped by one compact impenetrable body of ice. We ran along it from east to west above ten degrees, and on the 27th we got as far north as 80° 37'; and in 19 or 20 degrees east longitude from London. On 29 and 30 July we saw one continued plain of smooth unbroken ice, bounded only by the horizon, and we fastened to a piece of ice that was eight yards eleven inches thick. We had generally sunshine and constant daylight, which gave cheerfulness and novelty to the whole of this striking, grand, and uncommon scene; and to heighten it still more, the reflection of the sun from the ice gave the clouds a most beautiful appearance. We killed many different animals at this time, and among the rest nine bears. Though they had nothing in their paunches but water yet they were all very fat. We used to decoy them to the ship sometimes by burning feathers or skins. I thought them coarse eating, but some of the ship's company relished them very much. Some of our people once, in the boat, fired at and wounded a sea-horse, which dived immediately and in a little time after brought up with it a number of others. They all joined in an attack upon the boat and were with difficulty prevented from staving or oversetting her, but a boat from the *Carcass* having come to assist ours and joined it, they dispersed, after having wrested an oar from one of the men. One of the ship's boats had before been attacked in the same manner, but happily no harm was done. Though we wounded several of these animals we never got but one. We remained hereabouts until 1 August, when the two ships got completely fastened in the ice, occasioned by the loose ice that set in from the sea. This made our situation very dreadful and alarming, so that on the seventh day we were in very great apprehension of having the ships squeezed to pieces. The officers now held a council to know what was best for us to do in order to save our lives, and determined that we should endeavour to escape by dragging our boats along the ice towards the sea, which, however, was farther off than any of us thought. This determination filled us with extreme dejection and confounded us with despair, for we had very little prospect of escaping with life. However, we sawed some of the ice about the ships to keep it from hurting them, and thus kept them in a kind of pond. We then began to drag the boats as well as we could towards the sea, but after two or three days' labour we made very little progress, so that some of our hearts totally failed us and I really began to give up myself for lost when I saw our surrounding calamities. While we were at this hard labour I once fell into a pond we had made amongst some loose ice and was very near being drowned, but providentially some people were near who gave me immediate assistance and thereby I escaped drowning. Our deplorable condition, which kept up the constant apprehension of our perishing in the ice, brought me gradually to think of eternity in such a manner as I never had done before. I had the fears of death hourly upon me, and shuddered at the thoughts of meeting the grim king of terrors in the *natural* state I then was in, and was exceedingly doubtful of a happy eternity if I should die in it. I had no hopes of my life being prolonged for any time, for we saw that our existence could not be long on the ice after leaving the ships, which were now out of sight and some miles from the boats. Our appearance now became truly lamentable. Pale dejection seized every countenance. Many who had been before blasphemers, in this our distress began to call on the good God of Heaven for his help, and in the time of our utter need he heard us, and against hope or human probability delivered us! It was the eleventh day of the ships being thus fastened, and the fourth of our drawing the boats in this manner, that the wind changed to the E.N.E. The weather immediately became mild and the ice broke towards the sea, which was to the S.W. of us. Many of us on this got on board again, and with all our might we hove the ships into every open water we could find, and made all the sail on them in our power; and now, having a prospect of success, we made signals for the boats and the remainder of the people. This seemed to us like a reprieve from death, and happy was the man who could first get on board of any ship, or the first boat he could meet. We then proceeded in this manner till we got into the open water again, which we accomplished in about thirty hours to our infinite joy and gladness of heart. As soon as we were out of danger we came to anchor and refitted, and on 19 August we sailed from this uninhabited extremity of the world, where the inhospitable climate affords neither food nor shelter, and not a tree or shrub of any kind grows amongst its barren rocks, but all is one desolate and expanded waste of ice, which even the constant beams of the sun for six months in the year cannot penetrate or dissolve. The sun now being on the decline the days shortened as we sailed to the southward, and on the 28th in latitude 73°, it was dark by ten o'clock at night. September 10, in latitude 58°–59°, we met a very severe gale of wind and high seas, and shipped a great deal of water in the space of ten hours. This made us work exceedingly hard at all our pumps a whole day, and one sea which struck the ship with more force than anything I ever met with of the kind before, laid her under water for some time so that we thought she would have gone down. Two boats were washed from the booms, and the long-boat from the chucks: all other moveable things on the deck were also washed away, among which were many curious things of different kinds which we had brought from Greenland, and we were obliged in order to lighten the ship to toss some of our guns overboard. We saw a ship at the same time in very great distress, and her masts were gone, but we were unable to assist her. We now lost sight of the *Carcass* till the 26th, when we saw land about Orfordness, off which place she joined us. From thence we sailed for London and on the 30th came up to Deptford. And thus ended our Arctic voyage, to the no small joy of all on board, after having been absent four months; in which time, at the imminent hazard of our lives, we explored nearly as far towards the Pole as 81 degrees north, and 20 degrees east longitude, being much farther by all accounts than any navigator had ever ventured before, in which we fully proved the impracticability of finding a passage that way to India.

SPITSBERGEN or NEW GREENLAND.

N.E. Land

Seven Isles

Baltia Ships frozen up

Wyches Island

Foul Sound

Table Point

Olispe Island

Edge Mts

Cherry Isles

Iron Out P.t

Horn Sound

Fair Haven

Welt P.t

Curwate Outward Bound

Track of the Racehorse & C.

Bell Sound

Black P.t

Smeerenburg bay Harbour

Charles Isle

Hackluyts Headland

Deer Field

Red Point

Wygatz Straits

Phipps Headland

Homeward Bound

Meridian of London

the Ice

Track

P.t of John Mayen I.

Phipps' route to Spitsbergen

CHAPTER THIRTEEN

The Musquito Indians

I WAS happy once more amongst my friends and brethren till November, when my old friend the celebrated Doctor Irving bought a remarkable fine sloop, about 150 tons. He had a mind for a new adventure in cultivating a plantation at Jamaica and the Musquito Shore, asked me to go with him, and said that he would trust me with his estate in preference to anyone. By the advice therefore of my friends, I accepted of the offer, knowing that the harvest was full ripe in those parts, and hoped to be the instrument, under God, of bringing some poor sinner to my well beloved master, Jesus Christ. Before I embarked, I found with the Doctor four Musquito Indians who were chiefs in their own country and were brought here by some English traders for some selfish ends. One of them was the Musquito king's son, a youth of about eighteen years of age, and whilst he was here he was baptized by the name of George. They were going back at the government's expense after having been in England about twelve months, during which they learned to speak pretty good English. When I came to talk to them about eight days before we sailed, I was very much mortified in finding that they had not frequented any churches since they were here, to be baptized, nor was any attention paid to their morals. I was very sorry for this mock Christianity and had just an opportunity to take some of them once to church before we sailed. We embarked in the month of November 1775, on board of the sloop *Morning Star*, Captain David Miller, and sailed for Jamaica. In our passage I took all the pains that I could to instruct the Indian prince in the doctrines of Christianity, of which he was entirely ignorant, and to my great joy he was quite attentive and received with gladness the truths that the Lord enabled me to set forth to him. I taught him in the compass of eleven days all the letters, and he could put even two or three of them together and spell them. I had Fox's Martyrology with cuts, and he used to be very fond of looking into it, and would ask many questions about the papal cruelties he saw depicted there, which I explained to him. I made such progress with this youth, especially in religion, that when I used to go to bed at different hours of the night, if he was in his bed he would get up on purpose to go to prayer with me without any other clothes than his shirt, and before he would eat any of his meals amongst the gentlemen in the cabin, he would first come to me to pray, as he called it. I was well pleased at this and took great delight in him, and used much supplication to God for his conversion. I was in full hope of seeing daily every appearance of that change which I could wish, not knowing the devices of Satan, who had many of his emissaries to sow his tares as fast as I sowed the good seed, and pull down as fast as I built up. Thus we went on nearly four-fifths of our passage, when Satan at last got the upper hand. Some of his messengers, seing this poor heathen much advanced in piety, began to ask him whether I had converted him to Christianity, laughed and made their jest at him, for which I rebuked them as much as I could; but this treatment caused the prince to halt between two opinions. Some of the true sons of Belail, who did not believe that there was any hereafter, told him never to fear the devil, for there was none existing, and if ever he came to the prince, they desired he might be sent to them. Thus they teased the poor innocent youth, so that he would not learn his book any more! He would not drink nor carouse with these ungodly actors, not would he be with me, even at prayers. This grieved me very much. I endeavoured to persuade him as well as I could, but he would not come; and entreated him very much to tell me his reasons for acting thus. At last he asked me, 'How comes it that all the white men on board who can read and write, and observe the sun, and know all things, yet swear, lie, and get drunk, only excepting yourself?' I answered him, the reason was that they did not fear God, and that if anyone of them died so, they could not go to, or be happy with God. He replied that if these persons went to Hell he would go to Hell too. I was sorry to hear this, and as he sometimes had the toothache and also some other persons in the ship at the same time, I asked him if their toothache made his easy: he said, No. Then I told him if he and these people went to Hell together, their pains would not make his any lighter. This answer had great weight with him: it depressed his spirits much, and he became ever after, during the passage, fond of being alone. When we were in the latitude of Martinique and near making the land, one morning we had a brisk gale of wind, and, carrying too much sail, the mainmast went over the side. Many people were then all about the deck, and the yards, masts, and rigging came tumbling all about us, yet there was not one of us in the least hurt although some were within a hair's-breadth of being killed: and particularly, I saw two men then, by the providential hand of God, most miraculously preserved from being smashed to pieces. On 5 January we made Antigua and Montserrat and ran along the rest of the islands, and on the 14th we arrived at Jamaica. One Sunday while we were there I took the Musquito Prince George to church, where he saw the sacrament administered. When we came out we saw all kinds of people, almost from the church door for the space of half a mile down to the waterside, buying and selling all kinds of commodities, and these acts afforded me great matter of exhortation to this youth, who was much astonished. Our vessel being ready to sail for the Musquito shore, I went with the Doctor on board a Guinea-man, to purchase some slaves to carry with us and cultivate a plantation, and I chose them all from my own countrymen. On 12 February we sailed from Jamaica, and on the 18th arrived at the Musquito shore at a place called Dupeupy. All our Indian guests now, after I had admonished them and a few cases of liquor given them by the Doctor, took an affectionate leave of us and went ashore, where they were met by the Musquito king, and we never saw one of them afterwards. We then sailed to the southward of the shore, to a place called Cape Gracias a Dios, where there was a large lagoon or lake which received the emptying of two or three very fine large rivers and abounded much in fish and land tortoise. Some of the native Indians came on board of us here, and we used them well, and told them we were come to dwell amongst them, which they seemed pleased at. So the Doctor and I, with some others, went with them ashore, and they took us to different places to view the land in order to choose a place to make a plantation of. We fixed on a spot near a river's bank in a rich soil, and having got our necessaries out of the sloop, we began to clear away the woods and plant different kinds of vegetables which had a quick growth. While we were employed in this manner, our vessel went northward to Black River to trade. While she was there, a Spanish guarda costa met with her and took her. This proved very hurtful and a great embarrassment to us. However, we went on with the culture of the land. We used to make fires every night all around us to keep off wild beasts which, as soon as it was dark, set up a most hideous roaring. Our habitation being far up in the woods we frequently saw different kinds of animals, but none of them ever hurt us except poisonous snakes, the bite of which the Doctor used to cure by giving to the patient, as soon as possible, about half a tumbler of strong rum and a good deal of Cayenne pepper in it. In this manner he cured two natives and one of his own slaves. The Indians were exceedingly fond of the Doctor, and they had good reason for it, for I believe they never had such an useful man amongst them. They came from all quarters to our dwelling, and some *woolwow*, or flat-headed Indians, who lived fifty or sixty miles above our river and this side of the South Sea, brought us a good deal of silver in exchange for our goods. The principal articles we could get from our neighbouring Indians were turtle oil and shells, little silk grass, and some provisions, but they would not work at anything for us except fishing, and a few times they assisted to cut some trees down in order to build us houses, which they did exactly like the Africans by the joint labour of men women and children. I do not recollect any of them to have had more than two wives. These always accompanied their husbands when they came to our dwelling, and then they generally carried whatever they brought to us, and always squatted down behind their husbands. Whenever we gave them anything to eat, the men and their wives ate it separate. I never saw the least sign of incontinence amongst them. The women were ornamented with beads and fond of painting themselves. The men also paint, even to excess, both their faces and shirts: their favourite colour is red. The women generally cultivate the ground, and the men are all fishermen and canoe makers. Upon the whole, I never met any nation that were so simple in their manners as these people, or had so little ornament in their houses. Neither had they, as I ever could learn, one word expressive or an oath. The worst word I ever heard amongst them when they were quarrelling was one that they had got from the English, which was 'you rascal'. I never saw any mode of worship among them, but in this they were not worse than their European brethren or neighbours: for I am sorry to say that there was not one white person in our dwelling, nor anywhere else that I saw in different places I was at on the shore, that was better or more pious than those unenlightened Indians; but they either worked or slept on Sundays. And, to my sorrow, working was too much Sunday's employment with ourselves, so much so that in some length of time we really did not know one day from another. This mode of living laid the foundation of my decamping at last. The natives are well made and warlike, and they particularly boast of having never been conquered by the Spaniards. They are great drinkers of strong liquors when they can get them. We used to distil rum from pineapples, which were very plentiful here, and then we could not get them away from our place. Yet they seemed to be singular, in point of honesty, above any other nation I was ever amongst. The country being hot, we lived under an open shed where we had all kinds of goods, without a door or a lock to any one article, yet we slept in safety and never lost anything or were disturbed. This surprised us a good deal, and the Doctor, myself, and others, used to say if we were to lie in that manner in Europe we should have our throats cut the first night. The Indian governor goes once in a certain time all about the province or district, and has a number of men with him as attendants and assistants. He settles all the differences among the people, like the judge here, and is treated with very great respect. He took care to give us timely notice before he came to our habitation by sending his stick as a token, for rum, sugar, and gunpowder, which we did not refuse sending, and at the same time we made the utmost preparation to receive his honour and his train. When we came with his tribe and all our neighbouring chieftains, we expected to find him a grave reverend judge, solid and sagacious; but instead of that, before he and his gang came in sight we heard them very clamorous, and they even had plundered some of our good neighbouring Indians, having intoxicated themselves with our liquor. When they arrived we did not know what to make of our new guests and would gladly have dispensed with the honour of their company. However, having no alternative, we feasted them plentifully all the day till the evening, when the governor getting quite drunk, grew very unruly and struck one of our most friendly chiefs, who was our nearest neighbour, and also took his gold-laced hat from him. At this a great commotion took place, and the Doctor interfered to make peace as we could all understand one another, but to no purpose; and at last they became so outrageous that the Doctor, fearing he might get into trouble, left the house and made the best of his way to the nearest wood, leaving me to do as well as I could among them. I was so enraged with the Governor that I could have wished to have seen him tied fast to a tree and flogged for his behaviour, but I had not people enough to cope with his party. I therefore thought of a strategem to appease the riot. Recollecting a passage I had read in the life of Columbus when he was amongst the Indians in Mexico or Peru, where on some occasion he frightened them by telling them of certain events in the heavens, I had recourse to the same expedient, and it succeeded beyond my most sanguine expectations. When I had formed my determination I went in the midst of them, and, taking hold of the Governor, I pointed up to the heavens. I menaced him and the rest: I told them God lived there, and that he was angry with them, and they must not quarrel so; that they were all brothers, and if they did not leave off and go away quietly, I would take the book (pointing to the Bible), read, and *tell* God to make them dead. This was something like magic. The clamour immediately ceased and I gave them some rum and a few other things, after which they went away peaceably, and the Governor afterwards gave our neighbour who was called Captain Plasmyah, his hat again. When the Doctor returned he was exceedingly glad at my success in thus getting rid of our troublesome guests. The Musquito people within our vicinity, out of respect to the Doctor, myself and his people, made entertainments of the grand kind, called in their tongue *tourrie* or *dryckbot*. The English of this expression is a feast of drinking about, of which it seems a corruption of language. The drink consisted of pineapples roasted, and casades chewed or beaten in mortars, which, after lying some time, ferments and becomes so strong as to intoxicate when drank in any quantity. We had timely notice given to us of the entertainment. A white family within five miles of us told us how the drink was made, and I and two others went before the time to the village where the mirth was appointed to be held, and there we saw the whole art of making the drink and also the kind of animals that were to be eaten there. I cannot say the sight of either the drink or the meat were enticing to me. They had some thousands of pineapples roasting, which they squeezed, dirt and all, into a canoe they had there for the purpose. The casade drink was in beef barrels and other vessels and looked exactly like hog-wash. Men women and children were thus employed in roasting the pineapples and squeezing them with their hands. For food they had many land torpins or tortoises, some dried turtle, and three large alligators alive, and tied fast to the trees. I asked the people what they were going to do with these alligators, and I was told they were to be eaten. I was much surprised at this, and went home not a little disgusted at the preparations. When the day of the feast was come we took some rum with us and went to the appointed place, where we found a great assemblage of these people who received us very kindly. The mirth had begun before we came, and they were dancing with music. The musical instruments were nearly the same as those of any other sable people, but, as I thought, much less melodious than any other nation I ever knew. They had many curious gestures in dancing and a variety of motions and postures of their bodies which to me were in no wise attracting. The males danced by themselves, and the females also by themselves, as with us. The Doctor showed his people the example, by immediately joining the women's party, though not by their choice. On perceiving the women disgusted, he joined the males. At night there were great illuminations, by setting fire to many pine trees, while the *dryckbot* went round merrily by calabashes or gourds, but the liquor might more justly be called eating than drinking. One Owden, the oldest father in the vicinity, was dressed in a strange and terrifying form. Around his body were skins adorned with different kinds of feathers, and he had on his head a very large and high headpiece in the form of a grenadier's cap, with prickles like a porcupine, and he made a certain noise which resembled the cry of an alligator. Our people skipped amongst them out of complaisance, though some could not drink of their *tourrie*; but our rum met with customers enough and was soon gone. The alligators were killed and some of them roasted. Their manner of roasting is by digging a hole in the earth and filling it with wood, which they burn to coal, and then they lay sticks across on which they set the meat. I had a raw piece of the alligator in my hand. It was very rich. I thought it looked like fresh salmon, and it had a most fragrant smell, but I could not eat any of it. This merry-making at last ended without the least discord in any person in the company, although it was made up of different nations and complexions. The rainy season came on here about the latter end of May, which continued till August very heavily, so that the rivers were overflowed and our provisions then in the ground were washed away. I thought this was in some measure a judgement upon us for working on Sundays and it hurt my mind very much. I often wished to leave this place and sail for Europe, for our mode of procedure and living in this heathenish form was very irksome to me. The word of God saith, 'What does it avail a man if he gain the whole world, and lose his own soul?' This was much and heavily impressed on my mind, and though I did not know how to speak to the Doctor for my discharge, it was disagreeable for me to stay any longer. But about the middle of June I took courage enough to ask him for it. He was very unwilling at first to grant my request, but I gave him so many reasons for it that at last he consented to my going, and gave me the following certificate of my behaviour:

The bearer, Gustavus Vassa, has served me several years with strict honesty, sobriety, and fidelity. I can, therefore, with justice recommend him for these qualifications; and indeed in every respect I consider him an excellent servant. I do hereby certify that he always behaved well, and that he is perfectly trust-worthy.

CHARLES IRVING

Musquito Shore, June 15, 1767

Though I was much attached to the Doctor, I was happy when he consented. I got everything ready for my departure, and hired some Indians with a large canoe to carry me off. All my poor countrymen, the slaves, when they heard of my leaving them, were very sorry, as I had

always treated them with care and affection and did everything I could to comfort the poor creatures and render
their conditions easy. Having taken leave of my old friends
and companions, on 18 June, accompanied by the Doctor,
I left that spot of the world, and went southward above
twenty miles along the river. There I found a sloop, the
captain of which told me he was going to Jamaica. Having
agreed for my passage with him and one of the owners,
who was also on board, named Hughes, the Doctor and I
parted, not without shedding tears on both sides.

CHAPTER FOURTEEN

A Rough Road to Freedom

THE vessel then sailed along the river till night, when she stopped in a lagoon within the same river. During the night a schooner belonging to the same owners came in, and as she was in want of hands, Hughes, the owner of the sloop, asked me to go in the schooner as a sailor and said he would give me wages. I thanked him, but I said I wanted to go to Jamaica. He then immediately changed his tone, and swore and abused me very much, and asked how I came to be freed. I told him, and said that I came into that vicinity with Dr Irving, whom he had seen that day. This account was of no use. He still swore exceedingly at me, and cursed the master for a fool that sold me my freedom, and the Doctor for another in letting me go from him. Then he desired me to go in the schooner, or else I should not go out of the sloop as a freeman. I said this was very hard and begged to be put on shore again, but he swore that I should not. I said I had been twice amongst the Turks, yet had never seen any such usage with them, and much less could I have expected anything of this kind amongst Christians. This incensed him exceedingly, and with a volley of oaths and imprecations, he replied, 'Christians! Damn you, you are one of St Paul's men, but by G——, except you have St Paul's or St Peter's faith and walk upon the water to the shore, you shall not go out of the vessel,' which I now found was going amongst the Spaniards towards Carthagena, where he swore he would sell me. I simply asked him what right he had to sell me? But without another word he made some of his people tie ropes round each of my ankles and also to each wrist, and another rope round my body, and hoisted me up without letting my feet touch or rest upon anything. Thus I hung, without any crime committed and without judge or jury, merely because I was a free man and could not by the law get any redress from a white person in those parts of the world. I was in great pain from my situation and cried and begged very hard for some mercy, but all in vain. My tyrant, in a great rage, brought a musket out of the cabin and loaded it before me and the crew and swore that he would shoot me if I cried any more. I had now no alternative. I therefore remained silent, seeing not one white man on board who said a word on my behalf. I hung in that manner from between ten and eleven o'clock at night till about one in the morning when, finding my cruel abuser fast asleep, I begged some of his slaves to slack the rope that was round my body that my feet might rest on something. This they did at the risk of being cruelly used by their master, who beat some of them severely at first for not tying me when he commanded them. Whilst I remained in this condition till between five and six o'clock next morning, I trust I prayed to God to forgive this blasphemer who cared not what he did, but when he got up out of his sleep in the morning was of the very same temper and disposition as when he left me at night. When they got up the anchor and the vessel was getting under way, I once more cried and begged to be released, and now, being fortunately in the way of their hoisting the sails, they released me. When I was let down I spoke to one Mr Cox, a carpenter, whom I knew on board, on the impropriety of this conduct. He also knew the Doctor and the good opinion he ever had of me. This man

then went to the captain and told him not to carry me
away in that manner, that I was the Doctor's steward, who
regarded me very highly and would resent this usage when
he should come to know it. On which he desired a young
man to put me ashore in a small canoe I brought with me.
This sound gladdened my heart, and I got hastily into the
canoe and set off, whilst my tyrant was down in the cabin;
but he soon spied me out when I was not above thirty or
forty yards from the vessel, and running upon the deck
with a loaded musket in his hand he presented it at me and
swore heavily and dreadfully that he would shoot me that
instant if I did not come back on board. As I knew the
wretch would have done as he said without hesitation, I
put back to the vessel again; but as the good Lord would
have it, just as I was alongside he was abusing the captain
for letting me go from the vessel, which the captain returned
and both of them soon got into a very great heat. The young
man that was with me now got out of the canoe, the vessel
was sailing on fast with a smooth sea, and I then thought
it was neck or nothing, so at that instant I set off again for
my life in the canoe towards the shore, and fortunately the
confusion was so great amongst them on board that I got
out of the reach of the musket shot unnoticed, while the
vessel sailed on with a fair wind a different way, so that
they could not overtake me without tacking: but even
before that could be done I should have been on shore,
which I soon reached with many thanks to God for this
unexpected deliverance. I then went and told the other
owner, who lived near the shore, (with whom I had agreed
for my passage) of the usage I had met with. He was very
much astonished and appeared very sorry for it. After
treating me with kindness, he gave me some refreshment
and three heads of roasted Indian corn for a voyage of
about eighteen miles south, to look for another vessel. He
then directed me to an Indian chief of a district, who was

also the Musquito admiral and had once been at our dwelling, after which I set off with the canoe across a large lagoon alone (for I could not get anyone to assist me), though I was much jaded, and had pains in my bowels, by means of the rope I had hung by the night before. I was therefore at different times unable to manage the canoe, for the paddling was very laborious. However, a little before dark I got to my destined place, where some of the Indians knew me, and received me kindly. I asked for the admiral, and they conducted me to his dwelling. He was glad to see me and refreshed me with such things as the place afforded, and I had a hammock to sleep in. They acted towards me more like Christians than those whites I was amongst the last night, though they had been baptized. I told the admiral I wanted to go to the next port to get a vessel to carry me to Jamaica, and requested him to send the canoe back which I then had, for which I was to pay him. He agreed with me, and sent five able Indians with a large canoe to carry my things to my intended place, about fifty miles, and we set off the next morning. When we got out of the lagoon and went along shore, the sea was so high that the canoe was oftentimes very near being filled with water. We were obliged to go ashore and drag across different necks of land. We were also two nights in the swamps, which swarmed with mosquito flies, and they proved troublesome to us. This tiresome journey of land and water ended however on the third day, to my great joy, and I got on board of a sloop commanded by one Captain Jenning. She was then partly loaded and he told me he was expecting daily to sail for Jamaica, and having agreed with me to work my passage, I went to work accordingly. I was not many days on board before we sailed, but to my sorrow and disappointment, though used to such tricks, we went to the southward along the Musquito shore instead of steering for Jamaica.

I was compelled to assist in cutting a great deal of mahogany wood on the shore as we coasted along it and load the vessel with it before she sailed. This fretted me much, but as I did not know how to help myself among these deceivers, I thought patience was the only remedy I had left, and even that was forced. There was much hard work and little victuals on board, except by good luck we happened to catch turtles. On this coast there was also a particular kind of fish called manatee which is most excellent eating, and the flesh is more like beef than fish. The scales are as large as a shilling and the skin thicker than I ever saw that of any other fish. Within the brackish waters along shore there were likewise vast numbers of alligators which made the fish scarce. I was on board this sloop sixteen days, during which, in our coasting, we came to another place, where there was a smaller sloop called the *Indian Queen*, commanded by one John Baker. He also was an Englishman and had been a long time along the shore trading for turtle shells and silver, and had got a good quantity of each on board. He wanted some hands very much, and understanding I was a free man and wanted to go to Jamaica, he told me if he could get one or two, that he would sail immediately for that island. He also pretended to me some marks of attention and respect and promised to give me forty-five shillings sterling a month if I would go with him. I thought this much better than cutting wood for nothing. I therefore told the other captain that I wanted to go to Jamaica in the other vessel, but he would not listen to me, and seeing me resolved to go in a day or two he got the vessel to sail, intending to carry me away against my will. This treatment mortified me extremely. I immediately accordingly to an agreement I had made with the captain of the *Indian Queen*, called for her boat, which was lying near us, and it came alongside; and by the means of a North Pole shipmate which I met with in the sloop I was in,

I got my things into the boat and went on board of the
Indian Queen, 10 July. A few days after I was there, we got
all things ready and sailed, but again, to my great mortification, this vessel still went to the south, nearly as far as
Carthagena, trading along the coast instead of going to
Jamaica as the captain had promised me: and what was
worst of all, he was a very cruel and bloody-minded man,
and was a horrid blasphemer. Among others he had a white
pilot, one Stoker, whom he beat often as severely as he did
some negroes he had on board. One night in particular,
after he had beaten this man most cruelly, he put him into
the boat and made two negroes row him to a desolate key
or small island, and he loaded two pistols and swore
bitterly that he would shoot the negroes if they brought
Stoker on board again. There was not the least doubt but
that he would do as he said and the two poor fellows were
obliged to obey the cruel mandate, but when the captain
was asleep, the two negroes took a blanket and carried it
to the unfortunate Stoker, which I believe was the means of
saving his life from the annoyance of insects. A great deal
of entreaty was used with the captain the next day before
he would consent to let Stoker come on board, and when
the poor man was brought on board he was very ill from
his situation during the night, and he remained so till he
was drowned a little time after. As we sailed southward
we came to many uninhabited islands, which were over-
grown with fine large coconuts. As I was very much in
want of provisions, I brought a boatload of them on board
which lasted me and others for several weeks, and afforded,
us many a delicious repast in our scarcity.

On 14 October the *Indian Queen* arrived at Kingston in
Jamaica. When we were unloaded I demanded my wages,
which amounted to eight pounds and five shillings sterling,
but Captain Baker refused to give me one farthing although

it was the hardest-earned money I ever worked for in my life. I found our Doctor Irving upon this and acquainted him of the captain's knavery. He did all he could to help me to get my money and we went to every magistrate in Kingston (and there were nine), but they all refused to do anything for me, and said my oath could not be admitted against a white man. Nor was this all, for Baker threatened that he would beat me severely if he could catch me for attempting to demand my money, and this he would have done but that I got, by means of Dr Irving, under the protection of Captain Douglas of the *Squirrel* man-of-war. I thought this exceedingly hard usage, though indeed I found it to be too much the practice there to pay free men for their labour in this manner. One day I went with a free negro tailor named Joe Diamond to one Mr Cochran, who was indebted to him some trifling sun, and the man, not being able to get his money, began to murmur. The other immediately took a horse-whip to pay him with it, but by the help of a good pair of heels the tailor got off. Such oppressions as these made me seek for a vessel to get off the island as fast as I could, and by the mercy of God I found a ship in November bound for England, when I embarked with a convoy after having taken a last farewell of Doctor Irving. When I left Jamaica he was employed in refining sugars, and some months after my arrival in England I learned with much sorrow that this my amiable friend was dead, owing to his having eaten some poisoned fish. We had many very heavy gales of wind in our passage, in the course of which no material incident occurred, except that an American privateer, falling in with the fleet, was captured and set fire to by his Majesty's ship the *Squirrel*. On 7 January 1777, we arrived at Plymouth. I was happy once more to tread upon English ground, and after passing some little time at Plymouth and Exeter among some pious friends, whom I was happy to see, I went to London with a heart replete with thanks to God for all past mercies.

Such were the various scenes which I was a witness to and the fortune I experienced until the year 1777. Since that period my life has been more uniform and the incidents of it fewer than in any other equal number of years preceding; I therefore hasten to the conclusion of a narrative, which I fear the reader may think already sufficiently tedious.

I hope to have the satisfaction of seeing the renovation of liberty and justice resting on the British government, to vindicate the honour of our common nature. These are concerns which do not perhaps belong to any particular office: but, to speak more seriously to every man of sentiment, actions like these are the just and sure foundation of future fame; a reversion, though remote, is coveted by some noble minds as a substantial good. It is upon these grounds that I hope and expect the attention of gentlemen in power. These are designs consonant to the elevation of their rank and the dignity of their stations: they are ends suitable to the nature of a free and generous government; and, connected with views of empire and dominion, suited to the benevolence and solid merit of the legislature. It is a pursuit of substantial greatness. – May the time come – at least the speculation to me is pleasing – when the sable people shall gratefully commemorate the auspicious era of extensive freedom. Then shall those persons particularly be named with praise and honour, who generously proposed and stood forth in the cause of humanity, liberty, and good policy; and brought to the ear of the legislature designs worthy of royal patronage and adoption. May Heaven make the British senators the dispersers of light, liberty, and science, to the uttermost parts of the earth: then will be glory to God on the highest, on earth peace, and good-will to men: – Glory, honour, peace, etc. to every soul of man that worketh good, to the Britons first, (because to them the Gospel is preached) and also to the nations. 'Those that honour their Maker have mercy on the poor.' 'It is righteousness exalteth a nation; but sin is a reproach to any people; destruction shall be to the workers of iniquity, and the wicked shall fall by their own wickedness.' May the blessings of the Lord be upon the heads of all those who commiserated the cases of the oppressed negroes, and the fear of God prolong their days; and may their expectations be filled with gladness! 'The liberal devise liberal things, and by liberal things shall stand,' Isaiah xxxii. 8. They can say with pious Job, 'Did not I weep for him that was in trouble? was not my soul grieved for the poor?' Job xxx. 25.

As the inhuman traffic of slavery is to be taken into the consideration of the British legislature, I doubt not, if a system of commerce was established in Africa, the demand for manufactures would most rapidly augment, as the native inhabitants will insensibly adopt the British fashions, manners, customs, etc. In proportion to the civilization, so will be the consumption of British manufactures.

The wear and tear of a continent, nearly twice as large as Europe, and rich in vegetable and mineral production, is much easier conceived than calculated.

A case in point. It cost the Aborigines of Britain, little or nothing in clothing, etc. The difference between their forefathers and the present generation, in point of consumption, is literally infinite. The supposition is most obvious. It will be equally immense in Africa. The same cause, viz. civilization, will ever have the same effect.

It is trading upon safe grounds. A commercial intercourse with Africa opens an inexhaustible source of wealth to the manufacturing interests of Great Britain, and to all which the slave trade is an objection.

If I am not misinformed, the manufacturing interest is equal, if not superior, to the landed interest, as to the value, for reasons which will soon appear. The abolition of slavery, so diabolical, will give a most rapid extension of manufactures, which is totally and diametrically opposite to what some interested people assert.

The manufactures of this country must and will, in the nature and reason of things, have a full and constant employ by supplying the African markets.

Population, the bowels and surface of Africa, abound in valuable and useful returns; the hidden treasures of centuries will be brought to light and into circulation. Industry, enterprise, and mining, will have their full scope, proportionably as they civilize. In a word, it lays open an endless field of commerce to the British manufacturer and merchant adventurer. The manufacturing interest and the general interests are synonymous. The abolition of slavery would be in reality an universal good.

Tortures, murder, and every other imaginable barbarity and iniquity, are practised upon the poor slaves with impunity. I hope the slave trade will be abolished. I pray it may be an event at hand. The great body of manufacturers, uniting in the cause, will considerably facilitate and expedite it; and as I have already stated, it is most substantially their interest and advantage, and as such the nation's at large, (except those persons concerned in the manufacturing neck-yokes, collars, chains, handcuffs, leg-bolts, drags, thumb-screws, iron muzzles, and coffins; cats, scourges, and other instruments of torture used in the slave trade.) In a short time one sentiment alone will prevail, from motives of interest as well as justice and humanity. Europe contains one hundred and twenty millions of inhabitants. Query – How many millions doth Africa contain? Supposing the Africans, collectively and individually, to expend 5*l.* a head in raiment and furniture, yearly, when civilized, etc. an immensity beyond the reach of imagination!

This I conceive to be a theory founded upon facts, and therefore an infallible one. If the blacks were permitted to remain in their own country, they would double themselves every fifteen years. In proportion to such increase, will be the demand for manufactures. Cotton and indigo grow spontaneously in most parts of Africa; a consideration this of no small consequence to the manufacturing towns of Great Britain. It opens a most immense, glorious, and happy prospect – the clothing, etc. of a continent ten thousand miles in circumference, and immensely rich in productions of every denomination in return for manufactures.

I have only therefore to request the reader's indulgence and conclude. I am far from the vanity of thinking there is any merit in this narrative: I hope censure will be suspended when it is considered that it was written by one who was as unwilling as unable to adorn the plainness of truth by the colouring of imagination. My life and fortune have been extremely chequered and my adventures various. Even those I have related are considerably abridged. If any incident in this little work should appear uninteresting and trifling to most readers, I can only say as my excuse, for mentioning it that almost every event of my life made an impression on my mind and influenced my conduct. I early accustomed myself to look for the hand of God in the minutest occurrence and to learn from it a lesson of morality and religion, and in this light every circumstance I have related was to me of importance. After all, what makes any event important, unless by its observation we become better and wiser, and learn 'to do justly, to love mercy, and to walk humbly before God'? To those who are possessed of this spirit there is scarcely any book of incident so trifling that does not afford some profit, while to others the experience of ages seems of no use; and even to pour out to them the treasures of wisdom is throwing the jewels of instruction away.

Equiano's Appointment as Commissary for Stores

In November 1786, Equiano was appointed Commissary for Stores for the Black Poor going to Sierra Leone, but after he had quarrelled constantly with the Agent, Joseph Irwin, his appointment was terminated in March 1787, before the expedition left Plymouth for Sierra Leone.

The proposal to found a colony in Sierra Leone for freed slaves was made by Henry Smeathman in 1786. Smeathman was a botanist who had lived some years in Sierra Leone. A year before his proposals for the settlement of freed slaves he had given evidence before a commission that the climate of Sierra Leone would kill off a hundred convicts a month should a convict station be established there. But in 1786 he had plans of his own for the new colony, and so described its climate and fertility with enthusiasm. The Treasury and the Committee for the Relief of the Black Poor accepted his opinions about the suitability of Sierra Leone, but further investigations by the Committee revealed that Smeathman intended to set up estates there using local slave labour, and it looked as though the plans might be dropped. But Smeathman died, and the freed slaves themselves were eager to go to Sierra Leone, choosing Smeathman's friend Irwin themselves as his successor.

However, as the time approached for the sailing, doubts arose in the minds of the intending settlers. Some of them feared that they were being sent to a penal colony, others that they would be sold again as slaves. Ottobah Cugoano, a Fanti and former slave, writing in 1787, summarized their doubts and fears in his *Thoughts and Sentiments on the Evil of*

Slavery, the strongest being that of a return to enslavement. 'A burnt child dreads the fire', he wrote, and continued:

> For it seemed prudent and obvious to many of them taking heed of that sacred inquiry, *Doth a fountain send forth at the same place sweet water and bitter?* They were afraid that their doom would be to drink of the bitter water. For can it readily be conceived that government would establish a free colony for them nearly on the spot, while it supports its forts and garrisons to ensnare, merchandize, and to carry others into captivity and slavery? (*Thoughts* etc. pp. 141–2)

The result was that though many had agreed to travel on the expedition, few were now prepared to go, and the three ships prepared for the journey had to be filled up with anyone who could be persuaded to go aboard – this included a number of white prostitutes. It may be that these were among the passengers 'taken on contrary to my orders' about whom Equiano complained in the *Public Advertiser* of 14 July 1787, though there is no evidence to prove that the settlers were against their being taken aboard, and it seems likely that they were welcomed – there was a shortage of women amongst the settlers. Matters were further complicated by sickness and bad weather; a wait in Portsmouth for the sickness to clear up was followed by another wait at Plymouth while storm damage was repaired. Conditions on board were poor, and tempers became strained as a result of the delay. Equiano's quarrels with Irwin came to a head when he accused Irwin of embezzling funds and ill-treating the passengers, and was himself accused of insubordinate and insolent behaviour towards his superiors.

Equiano wrote a letter at this time to Cugoano, which was published in the *Public Advertiser* on 4 April 1787. He wrote: 'I am sorry you and some more are not here with us. I am sure Irwin, and Fraser the Parson, are great villains, and Dr Currie. I am exceeding much grieved at the conduct of those who call themselves gentlemen. They now mean to serve (or use) the blacks the same as they do in the West Indies.' He went on to say that the stories accusing him of causing trouble between white and black were false 'for I am the greatest peacemaker that goes out'. Captain Thompson of the *Nautilus* had been asked by him to investigate and 'see the wrongs done to me and the people: so Capt. Thompson came and saw it and ordered the things to be given according to contract – which is not done yet in many things – and many of the black people have died for want of their due . . . I do not know how this undertaking will end; I wish I had never been involved with it; but at times I think the Lord will make me very useful at last.' An extract from a letter by another educated African, A. E. Griffith, was also printed in this issue of the *Public Advertiser*. 'The people, in general, are very sickly,' said Griffith, 'and die very fast indeed, for the doctors are very neglectful to the people, very much so.'

Counter-charges were made. In the *Public Advertiser* of 14 April, Equiano was accused of 'advancing falsehoods as deeply black as his jetty face'. He was said to have incited the settlers to mutiny, to have turned black against white, to have been insolent in his manner. 'No man endowed with common sense,' the writer continued, 'can credit for a moment that the Committee (all men of acknowledged humanity and honour) would give any countenance to the least ill-treatment of the objects of their compassion, whom they have endeavoured to snatch from misery and place in comfortable situations. . . . The proceedings of the Committee do them the greatest honour, and as Christians they have provided for the poor blacks every necessary of life, and will on their arrival in Sierra Leone place them in such a situation as to enable them to live happily.'

In fact, the expedition was little short of disastrous. Because of the delays in sailing, the ships reached Sierra Leone just before the rains, which were particularly heavy that year: the tents were inadequate, planting was impossible, and sickness continued to kill off the disheartened settlers so that within three months a third of them had died. It is difficult to place the blame – it was placed upon the inadequate diet and degenerate lives of the settlers, but the reasons were more complex than this. However, Equiano's doubts about the expedition appear to have been justified by its subsequent failure.

At the time, there was a considerable body of opinion against Equiano, for in addition to his enemies, both Captain Thompson and Granville Sharp, the leading figure of the abolitionist movement, criticized him. Granville Sharp wrote to his brother in June 1787 that 'all the jealousies and animosities between the Whites and the Blacks had subsided, and that they had been very orderly since Mr Vasa and two or three other discontented persons had been left on shore at Plymouth.' (P. Hoare, *Memoir of Granville Sharp*: London 1820, p. 313). He presumably got this information in letters from the expedition written at Tenerife, for similar remarks were made by the Rev. Fraser ('Fraser the Parson') in a letter quoted by the *Public Advertiser* on 2 July 1787, in which he accused Equiano of urging the settlers to stay away from his religious services 'for no other reason whatever than that I am *white*'. Captain Thompson, too, wrote an unfavourable report of Equiano to the Navy Board, calling him 'turbulent and discontented, taking every means to actuate the minds of the blacks to discord' – though he added 'I am equally chagrined to say that I do not find Mr Irwin the least calculated to conduct this business: as I have never observed any wish of his to facilitate the sailing of the ships, or any steps taken by him which might indicate that he had the welfare of the people the least at heart'. (P.R.O. T.i/643, 681)

On the other hand, the Navy Board did not accept Captain Thompson's judgement of Equiano, and forwarded Thompson's letter with these additional comments: 'We . . . desire you will please to acquaint the Right Honble. the Lords Commiss. of the Treasury that in all the Transactions the Commissary has had with this Board he has acted with great propriety and been very regular in his information but having from the beginning expressed his suspicions of Mr Irwin's intentions in supplying Tea, Sugar and other Necessaries allowed for the use of the Women and Children on their Passage and having complained from time to time of his conduct in this particular. We are not surprised at the disagreement that has taken place between them.' (P.R.O. T. i/643, 681) The Navy Board were more inclined to blame the trouble on the delays, and the temptations offered by the port to the restless and discontented settlers. Ultimately, the award of L.50 to Equiano in payment for his services indicated that he was still viewed favourably by the authorities, and he appears to have remained on good terms with the Abolitionist leaders. Although Granville Sharp criticised him at the time of the Sierra Leone expedition, he visited Equiano on his deathbed, and could call him 'an honest, sober man'. The many editions of Equiano's book were strongly supported by the Abolitionist movement, if we are to judge by the names on the subscription lists. Equiano continued to speak with affection and respect of Sharp, Clarkson and others. And the testimonials given to Equiano by such men as Thomas Clarkson and Dr Peckard on his journeys through Britain after 1789 are all very favourable – typical is one from Thomas Digges in Ireland who wrote of him that 'he supported an irreproachable character and was a principal instrument in bringing about the motion for a repeal of the Slave-act'. (*Interesting Narrative* 1793 – sixth edition.)

Equiano's own Account of the Affair from Chapter 12 of his Book

On my return to London in August I was very agreeably surprised to find that the benevolence of government had adopted the plan of some philanthropic individuals to send the Africans from hence to their native quarter; and that some vessels were then engaged to carry them to Sierra Leone; an act which redounded to the honour of all concerned in its promotion, and filled me with prayers and much rejoicing. There was then in the city a select committee of gentlemen for the black poor, to some of whom I had the honour of being known; and, as soon as they heard of my arrival they sent for me to the committee. When I came there they informed me of the intention of government; and as they seemed to think me qualified to superintend part of the undertaking, they asked me to go with the black poor to Africa. I pointed out to them many objections to my going; and particularly I expressed some difficulties on the account of the slave dealers, as I would certainly oppose their traffic in the human species by every means in my power. However these objections were over-ruled by the gentlemen of the committee, who prevailed on me to go, and recommended me to the honourable Commissioners of his Majesty's Navy as a proper person to act as commissary for government in the intended expedition; and they accordingly appointed me in November 1786 to that office, and gave me sufficient power to act for the government in the capacity of commissary, having received my warrant and the following order.

By the principal Officers and Commissioners of his Majesty's Navy.

Whereas you were directed, by our warrant of the 4th of last month, to receive into your charge from Mr Irving the surplus provisions remaining of what was provided for the voyage, as well as the provisions for the support of the black poor, after the landing at Sierra Leone, with the clothing, tools, and all other articles provided at government's expense; and as the provisions were laid in at the rate of two months for the voyage, and for four months after the landing, but the number embarked being so much less than was expected, whereby there may be a considerable surplus of provisions, clothing, etc. These are, in addition to former orders, to direct and require you to appropriate or dispose of such surplus to the best advantage you can for the benefit of government, keeping and rendering to us a faithful account of what you do herein. And for your guidance in preventing any white persons going, who are not intended to have the indulgence of being carried thither, we send you herewith a list of those recommended by the Committee for the black poor as proper persons to be permitted to embark, and acquaint you that you are not to suffer any others to go who do not produce a certificate from the committee for the black poor, of their having their permission for it. For which this shall be your warrant. Dated at the Navy Office, January 16, 1787.

J. HINSLOW,
GEO. MARSH,
W. PALMER.

To Mr. Gustavus Vassa,
  Commissary of Provisions and Stores for the Black Poor going to Sierra Leone.

I proceeded immediately to the execution of my duty on board the vessels destined for the voyage, where I continued till the March following.

During my continuance in the employment of government, I was struck with the flagrant abuses committed by the agent, and endeavoured to remedy them, but without effect. One instance, among many which I could produce, may serve as a specimen. Government had ordered to be provided all necessaries (slops, as they are called, included) for 750 persons; however, not being able to muster more than 426, I was ordered to send the superfluous slops, etc. to the king's stores at Portsmouth; but, when I demanded them for that purpose from the agent, it appeared they had never been bought, though paid for by government. But that was not all, government were not the only objects of peculation; these poor people suffered infinitely more; their accommodations were most wretched; many of them wanted beds, and many more clothing and other necessaries. For the truth of this, and much more, I do not seek credit from my own assertion. I appeal to the testimony of Capt. Thompson, of the *Nautilus*, who convoyed us, to whom I applied in February 1787 for a remedy, when I had remonstrated to the agent in vain, and even brought him to be a witness of the injustice and oppression I complained of. I appeal also to a letter written by these wretched people, so early as the beginning of the preceding January, and published in the *Morning Herald* of the 4th of that month, signed by twenty of their chiefs.

I could not silently suffer government to be thus cheated, and my countrymen plundered and oppressed, and even left destitute of the necessaries for almost their existence. I therefore informed the Commissioners of the Navy of the agent's proceedings; but my dismission was soon after procured, by means of a gentleman in the city, whom the agent, conscious of his peculation, had deceived by letter, and whom, moreover, empowered the same agent to receive on board, at the government's expense, a number of persons as passengers, contrary to the orders I received. By this I suffered a considerable loss in my property: however, the commissioners were satisfied with my conduct, and wrote to Capt. Thompson, expressing their approbation of it.

Thus provided, they proceeded on their voyage; and at last, worn out by treatment, perhaps not the most mild, and wasted by sickness, brought on by want of medicine, clothes, bedding, etc. they reached Sierra Leone just at the commencement of the rains. At that season of the year it is impossible to cultivate the lands; their provisions therefore were exhausted before they could derive any benefit from agriculture; and it is not surprising that many, especially the lascars, whose constitutions are very tender, and who had been cooped up in ships from October to June, and accommodated in the manner I have mentioned, should be so wasted by their confinement as not long to survive it.

Thus ended my part of the long-talked-of expedition to Sierra Leone; an expedition which, however unfortunate in the event, was humane and politic in its design, nor was its failure owing to government: everything was done on their part; but there was evidently sufficient mismanagement attending the conduct and execution of it to defeat its success.

I should not have been so ample in my account of this transaction, had not the share I bore in it been made the subject of partial animadversion, and even my dismission from my employment thought worthy of being made by some a matter of public triumph. The motives which might influence any person to descend to a petty contest with an obscure African, and to seek gratification by his depression, perhaps it is not proper here to inquire into or relate, even if its detection were necessary to my vindication; but I thank Heaven it is not. I wish to stand by my own integrity, and not to shelter myself under the impropriety of another; and I trust the behaviour of the Commissioners of the Navy to me entitle me to make this assertion; for after I had been dismissed, March 24, I drew up a memorial thus:

To the Right Honourable the Lords Commissioners of his Majesty's Treasury:

The Memorial and Petition of GUSTAVUS VASSA *a black Man, late Commissary to the black Poor going to* AFRICA.

HUMBLY SHEWETH,

That your Lordships' memorialist was, by the Honourable the Commissioners of his Majesty's Navy, on the 4th of December last, appointed to the above employment by warrant from that board;

That he accordingly proceeded to the execution of his duty on board of the *Vernon*, being one of the ships appointed to proceed to Africa with the above poor;

That your memorialist, to his great grief and astonishment, received a letter of dismission from the Honourable Commissioners of the Navy, by your Lordships' orders;

That, conscious of having acted with the most perfect fidelity and the greatest assiduity in discharging the trust reposed in him, he is altogether at a loss to conceive the reasons of your Lordships' having altered the favourable opinion you were pleased to conceive of him, sensible that your Lordships' would not proceed to so severe a measure without some apparent good cause; he therefore has every reason to believe that his conduct has been grossly misrepresented to your Lordships; and he is the more confirmed in his opinion, because, by opposing measures of others concerned in the same expedition, which tended to defeat your Lordships' humane intentions, and to put the government to a very considerable additional expense, he created a number of enemies, whose misrepresentations, he has too much reason to believe, laid the foundation of his dismission. Unsupported by friends, and unaided by the advantages of a liberal education, he can only hope for redress from the justice of his cause, in addition to the mortification of having been removed from his employment, and the advantage which he reasonably might have expected to have derived therefrom. He has had the misfortune to have sunk a considerable part of his little property in fitting himself out, and in other expenses arising out of his situation, an account of which he here annexes. Your memorialist will not trouble your Lordships with a vindication of any part of his conduct, because he knows not of what crimes he is accused; he, however, earnestly entreats that you will be pleased to direct an inquiry into his behaviour during the time he acted in the public service; and, if it be found that his dismission arose from false representations, he is confident that in your Lordships' justice he shall find redress.

Your petitioner therefore humbly prays that your Lordships will take his case into consideration, and that you will be pleased to order payment of the above referred-to account, amounting to 32l. 4s. and also the wages intended, which is most humbly submitted.

London, May 12, 1787.

The above petition was delivered into the hands of their Lordships, who were kind enough, in the space of some few months afterwards, without hearing, to order me 50l. sterling – that is, 18l. wages for the time (upwards of four months) I acted a faithful part in their service. Certainly the sum is more than a free negro would have had in the western colonies!!!

Miscellaneous Verses

or

Reflections on the State of my mind during my first Convictions; of the Necessity of believing the Truth, and experiencing the inestimable Benefits of Christianity.

Well may I say my life has been
One scene of sorrow and of pain;
From early days I griefs have known,
And as I grew my griefs have grown:

Dangers were always in my path;
And fear of wrath, and sometimes death;
While pale dejection in me reign'd
I often wept, by grief constrain'd.

When taken from my native land,
By an unjust and cruel band,
How did uncommon dread prevail!
My sighs no more I could conceal.

To ease my mind I often strove,
And tried my trouble to remove:
I sung, and utter'd sighs between –
Assay'd to stifle guilt with sin.

But O! not all that I could do
Would stop the current of my woe;
Conviction still my vileness shew'd;
How great my guilt – how lost from God!

Prevented, that I could not die,
Nor might to one kind refuge fly;
An orphan state I had to mourn –
Forsook by all, and left forlorn.

Those who beheld my downcast mien
Could not guess at my woes unseen:
They by appearance could not know
The troubles that I waded through.

Lust, anger, blasphemy, and pride,
With legions of such ills beside,
Troubled my thoughts while doubts and fears
Clouded and darken'd most my years.

Sighs now no more would be confin'd –
They breath'd the trouble of my mind:
I wish'd for death, but check'd the word,
And often pray'd unto the Lord.

Unhappy, more than some on earth,
I thought the place that gave me birth –
Strange thoughts oppress'd – while I replied
'Why not in Ethiopia died?'

And why thus spared, nigh to hell? –
God only knew – I could not tell!
A tott'ring fence, a bowing wall,
I thought myself e'er since the fall.

Oft times I mused, nigh despair,
While birds melodious fill'd the air:
Thrice happy songsters, ever free,
How bless'd were they compar'd to me!

Thus all things added to my pain,
While grief compell'd me to complain;
When sable clouds began to rise
My mind grew darker than the skies.

The English nation call'd to leave,
How did my breast with sorrows heave!
I long'd for rest – cried 'Help me, Lord!
Some mitigation, Lord, afford!'

Yet on, dejected, still I went –
Heart-throbbing woes within were pent;
Nor land, nor sea, could comfort give,
Nothing my anxious soul relieve.

Weary with travail, yet unknown
To all but God and self alone,
Numerous months for peace I strove
And numerous foes I had to prove.

Inur'd to dangers, griefs, and woes,
Train'd up 'midst perils, deaths, and foes,
I said 'Must it thus ever be? –
No quiet is permitted me.'

Hard hap, and more than heavy lot!
I pray'd to God 'Forget me not –
What thou ordain'st willing I'll bear
But O! deliver from despair!'

Strivings and wrestlings seem'd in vain;
Nothing I did could ease my pain:
Then gave I up my works and will,
Confess'd and own'd my doom was hell!

Like some poor pris'ner at the bar,
Conscious of guilt, of sin and fear,
Arraign'd, and self-condemn'd I stood –
Lost in the world, and in my blood!

Yet here, 'midst blackest clouds confin'd,
A beam from Christ, the day-star, shin'd;
Surely, thought I, if Jesus please,
He can at once sign my release.

I, ignorant of his righteousness,
Set up my labours in its place;
Forgot for why his blood was shed,
And pray'd and fasted in its stead.

He dy'd for sinners – I am one!
Might not his blood for me atone?
Tho' I am nothing else but sin,
Yet surely he can make me clean!

Thus light came in and I believ'd;
Myself forgot, and help receiv'd!
My Saviour then I know I found,
For, eas'd from guilt, no more I groan'd.

O happy hour, in which I ceas'd
To mourn, for then I found a rest!
My soul and Christ were now as one –
Thy light, O Jesus, in me shone!

Bless'd by thy name, for now I know
I and my works can nothing do;
The Lord alone can ransom man –
For this the spotless Lamb was slain!

When sacrifices, works, and pray'r,
Prov'd vain, and ineffectual were,
'Lo, then I come!' the Saviour cry'd,
And, bleeding, bow'd his head and dy'd!

He dy'd for all who ever saw
No help in them, nor by the law: –
I this have seen; and gladly own
'Salvation is by Christ alone*!'

* Acts iv, 12

APPENDIX III

London Feby the 27.th———1792

Dr. Revd. & Worthy friends &c.

This with my Best of Respects to you and wife with many
Prayers that you both may ever be Well in Souls and Bodys———
5 & also your Little Lovely Daughter———I thank you for all kind-
nesses which you was please to show me, may God ever Reward
you for it———Sir, I went to Ireland & was there 8½ months———
& sold 1900 copies of my narrative. I came here on the 10th inst.
———& I now mean as it seem Pleasing to my Good God!———
10 to leave London in about 8———or 10 Days more, & take me a
Wife———(one Miss Cullen———) of Soham in Cambridge shire
———& when I have given her about 8 or 10 Days Comfort, I
mean Directly to go to Scotland———and sell my 5th. Editions
———I Trust that my going about has been of much use to the
15 Cause of the Abolition of the accu[r]sed Slave Trade———a
Gentleman of the Committee the Revd. Dr. Baker has said that
I am more use to the Cause than half the People in the Country
———I wish to God, I could be so. a noble Earl of Stanhope has
Lately Consulted me twice about a Bill which his Ld.ship now
20 mean to bring in to the House to allow the sable People of the wt
Indias the Rights of taking an oath against any White Person
———I hope it may Pass, tis high time———& will be of much use.
———May the Lord Bless all the friends of Humanity. Pray
Pardon what ever you here see amiss———I will be Glad to see
25 you at my Wedg.———Pray give my best Lcve To the Worthy
& Revd. Mr. Robinson, & his———also to my friends Coltman
———and Mr. & Mrs. Buxton———I Pray that the Good Lord
may make all of that family Rich in faith as in the things of this
World———I have Great Deal to say if I ever have the Pleasure
30 to see you again———I have been in the uttermust hurry ever
since I have being in this wickd. Town———& I only came now
to save if I can, £232, I Lent to a man, who now Dying. Pray
Excuse ha[ste]———will be Glad to hear from you———& do very
much beg your Prayers as you ever have mine———& if I see you

35 no more here Below may I see you all at Last at Gods Right
Hand——where parting will be no more——Glory to God
that J. Christ is yet all, & in all, to my Poor Soul——
     I am with all Due Respects
        yours to Command——
40   Gustavus Vassa
                The African
     ——————at Mr. Hardys No. 4 Taylors Building
                Chandos street, Covent Garden
     [Reverse side]
45 P.S. you see how I am confused——Pray excuse this mistake
   of the frank——
   for Mr. Housman
   Pray mind the Africans from the Pulpits

Notes

Chapter One

page
  1 *That part of Africa:* Equiano refers several times in footnotes
    to Anthony Benezet's *Some Historical Account of Guinea*, to
    support his statements about African society and the slave
    trade. There are occasional verbal echoes of Benezet, as in
    the opening sentence of this volume—compare Benezet:
        That part of Africa from which the Negroes are to be
        sold into slavery, commonly known by the name of
        Guinea, extends along the coast some three or four
        thousand miles. (1788 edition p. 5.)
    Equiano may have found support for his economic ideas
    in Benezet, too–see the note on *A system of commerce*, p. 198.
  1 *The Kingdom of Benin . . . Abyssinia:* the Benin Empire
    stretched westwards beyond Lagos and north as far as Idah.
    To the east its power was not directly effective beyond the
    Niger, though Dike writes of 'the powerful influence which
    this kingdom exerted over the imagination of her neigh-
    bours, particularly in south-eastern Nigeria, where her
    power was felt by Ibos and Ibo-speaking peoples east of the
    Niger'. (K. Dike, *Trade and Politics in the Niger Delta*, Oxford

University Press, 1956, p. 21.) Some such tradition would
explain the otherwise puzzling claim by Equiano that his
people were subject to the Kingdom of Benin. Equiano
exaggerates its size, when he says that it extends 1,500 miles
into the interior. But his remarks may do no more than
reflect the almost fabulous reputation of Benin, possibly
carried to his home by traders from the Niger such as the
'Oye-Eboe' on page 7.

1 *The line:* the Equator.

1 *Essaka:* this has been impossible to identify, but Equiano's
account of his journey to the coast indicates that it must
have been well into the interior, and to the east of the Niger.
The likeliest part is somewhere south-east of Onitsha and
north of Owerri, though if the 'large river' (see p. 23) were
to have been the Niger Delta rather than the River Niger,
Essaka might have been further east still. But even if we
could be confident of the accuracy of Equiano's account of
his journey, which we cannot, it would still be difficult to
locate Essaka with any certainty.

2 *Embrenché:* John Adams, an early nineteenth-century
writer, in *Sketches* (London, 1822, pp. 41–42), says that the
Ibo word for 'gentleman' is *Breeché*; this appears to be the
same word as Equiano's *Embrenché*. It has been suggested
that this is the modern Ibo *ndichi*, the name given to titled
men (C. K. Meek, *Law and Authority in a Nigerian Tribe*,
Oxford University Press, 1937, p. 7). But more likely is
mgburichi, a name given in parts of Ibo to men bearing scars
like those described. They are mentioned by J. Africanus
Horton in his *West African Countries and Peoples* (London,
1868, p. 178) when, describing similar markings made at
Isuama, he says 'The people so tattooed are called
Mbritshi or Itshi'.

2 *Adultery:* feelings are not usually so strong on this subject
in modern Ibo society, and fines or the payment of com-
pensation are the usual penalties. But adultery within the
kinship group, which is probably what Equiano refers to,
was often punished in the past by death or enslavement
(Meek, p. 218f.) and has been treated as a serious matter
in modern times. Green was told that 'when the old penalty
(i.e. burial alive) cannot be carried out, if people knew of a
case occurring, they would go out at night and kill the man
and put his body under a palm tree. The British authorities

would then think he had fallen and killed himself while climbing for palm-nuts.' (M. M. Green, *Ibo Village Affairs*, Sidgwick and Jackson, 1947, p. 100.)

2 *Marriage*: a detailed and accurate account of marriage customs could hardly be expected of a forty-year-old man describing a society he had left at the age of ten, but in general the customs here resemble those of modern times. There is no modern custom which resembles the tying on of the cotton string at marriage, and Equiano may be confusing this with the εmε, tied round a girl's waist at puberty. Talbot makes reference to some such custom – 'they were formerly allowed to wear nothing but a cotton string or circlet of brass wire called Awna-ididi after puberty, and a very small loin cloth after marriage' he writes of the women in one part of Ibo. (P. A. Talbot, *The Peoples of Southern Nigeria*, Vol. II, Oxford University Press, 1926, p. 405.)

3 *Dancing*: in modern times, though custom varies, generally speaking dancers would separate into four main groups – men, boys, married women, and girls. With regard to the style of dancing, Equiano adds the note: 'When I was in Smyrna I have frequently seen the Greeks dance after this manner.' The resemblance of Greek to West African dancing is mentioned in the *Encyclopedia of Religion and Ethics*, ed. J. Hastings, Edinburgh, 1911, in the entry on Processions and Dancing. Edward Blyden, travelling in Syria in the 1860s, noted the resemblance between West African dances and those of Syria. (*From West Africa to Jerusalem*, Freetown, 1873, p. 146.)

4 *Instruments*: both the 'guitar' (θbɔ) and the stickado or xylophone (ngɛlɛngɛ) are still played by the Ibos. The xylophone is not, however, played normally by young women.

4 *Dye*: the most common blue dye would be indigo, but this is extracted from the leaves, not the berries of the plant. However, there are several berries giving a blue dye to be found in Nigeria.

4 *Tobacco pipes*: pipe smoking is very popular amongst the Ibos, but the pipe (ɔkpɔkɔ) is short. Long pipes are smoked in the north of Nigeria, and I have been told that they are found sometimes in Ibo. Equiano's note describing the pipe is as follows: 'The bowl is earthen, curiously figured, to which a long reed is fixed as a tube. The tube is sometimes

so long as to be borne by one, and frequently out of grandeur, two boys.' Writing of the Fanti of the Gold Coast,
John Adams (*Sketches Taken During Ten Voyages etc.*, London,
1822, p. 8) refers to 'the boy who carries the smoking
apparatus belonging to a gentleman'.

5 *Salt:* this was a principal item of trade at this time, and
was commonly extracted from wood or leaves. Crow's
Memoirs mention salt made at Bonny 'from the green man-
grove bushes which are burned in large brass pans.' (H.
Crow, *Memoirs*, London, 1830, p. 250) and another description is to be found in Dike, *op. cit.*, p. 22. A salt used in
the fixing of dye is obtained by burning Ironwood (Talbot,
op. cit., Vol. III, p. 942).

5 *Eadas:* probably eddoes, a West Indian name for coco-
yam, sometimes spelt 'eddas' in the eighteenth century.
The Ibo word is εdo.

5 *Palm-wine:* in comparison with the eighteenth century gin-
drinker, Equiano's palm-wine drinkers may well have
appeared sober, but he does rather underestimate the
intoxicating powers of palm-wine.

5 *Scented wood and earth:* the wood appears to be Camwood,
which is prepared in the way described for smearing on the
body ceremonially, but it does not have the strong, pleasant
scent described here. I can give no explanation of the earth
which gives off a scent when placed on the fire. Equiano
says in a note that he came across the same kind of powder
in Smyrna – this was probably some such preparation as
the Persian *ambar*, a powder which gives a sweet smell
when burnt.

6 *Cow dung:* Adams writes of the use of cow dung in this way
by the natives of Ardra (pp. 20–21), saying that it 'has by
no means an unpleasant smell, and fills up crevices, which
would otherwise be tenanted by noxious and troublesome
insects.' Talbot mentions its use in Ibo houses (*op cit.*, Vol.
III, p. 881) though it is a common practice in many parts
of Africa.

6 *Coins:* Talbot records the use amongst the Ibo of 'small
pieces of iron in the shape of fishhooks' (Talbot III, p. 876)
and these are presumably the same as the '*umumu* currency,
consisting of tiny arrow-shaped pieces of iron' still found
in the eastern Onitsha region (Daryll Forde and G. J.
Jones, *The Ibo and Ibibio-speaking Peoples of South-Eastern*

Nigeria, Oxford University Press, 1950, p. 15).

7 *Oye-Eboe:* the word *oyibo* is used in Ibo for white men, and is a borrowing from Yoruba. But it has been suggested by Chinua Achebe that the word Equiano uses here is the modern *onye Igbo*, meaning simply 'Ibo-man', since in the past the name *Igbo* was applied to 'the next clan'. A further suggestion is that 'Eboe' here is the modern Aboh, on the Niger below Onitsha, which was in the past sometimes called 'Ebo'. The rulers of Aboh gained their authority from the Kings of Benin, and only a few years before the birth of Equiano 'two claimants to the stool at Ebo (Aboh) appealed to the Oba as their overlord to decide who was the rightful heir'. (J. E. Egharevba, *A Short History of Benin*, Ibadan, 1960, p. 41.) If the Oye-Eboe were 'Aboh-men' it might explain how the reputation of Benin was carried inland to Equiano's home.

7 *Sugar-loaf:* a cone-shaped cake of refined sugar.

8 *Planters prefer . . . the slaves of Benin and Eboe:* Equiano's patriotism is not particularly well supported by testimony. One planter is recorded in Sir Alan Burns' *History of the British West Indies* as saying that he would rather give L.40 for a Gold Coast slave than L.20 for one from Calabar. (See p. 492, also p. 55). In fact, apart from slaves from Popo, who were also very highly regarded, Gold Coast slaves had the best reputation.

9 *Women warriors:* at first sight, this seems unlikely. The women of the Ibo are traditionally the peacemakers, and Green writes that 'in war it is the function of the women to override the fighting of the men and make peace . . . the female principle seems to be, in general, associated with a cooling, pacifying influence'. (Green, p. 177, and again p. 256) Equiano repeats this statement however (I.70 in the 1789 edition), saying that the women wherever he travelled from his home to the coast were 'trained in the arts of war'. The only West African tradition of women warriors is of the 'Amazons' of the King of Dahomey, but it may have been that, in times of danger, the women had to be prepared to help their men. Adams observed of the Ibibios, early in the nineteenth century, that the women were 'equally mischievous and ferocious as the men' (Adams, *op. cit.*, p. 140). And the Ibo women in more recent times have shown that they are no weaklings. 'The widespread

riots of 1929 will long stand as an example of the unity, power and determination which Ibo women can display. (Forde and Jones, *op. cit.*, p. 24). Horton (*op. cit.*, p. 179) quotes Samuel Crowther as recording that the Ibo women follow the men to their battles 'and are employed in removing the dead and wounded out of the way'. There is also an Ibo legend which tells that God decided not to allow women to fight wars, since they were so fierce that they might have wiped out the world.

10 *Slavery:* the distinction which Equiano makes here between domestic slavery in Africa and the slave trade is one which has been generally recognized by historians as valid. Without idealizing the lot of the domestic slave in Africa, it is apparent that they did not normally suffer the degradation of the West Indian slaves, and could often achieve eminence in their society. Thus, for instance, King Ja-Ja of Opobo and Kauran Chachi the warrior leader of Abuja both rose from slavery.

10 *Creator:* this appears to be the supreme god of the Ibos, Chukwu. He is often said to live in the sun, or is identified with Anyanwu the Sun. (Meek, p. 21, Talbot, Vol. II, p. 43, Forde and Jones, p. 25). The statement that he does not eat or drink may reflect the rarity of direct sacrifices to him. (Forde and Jones, p. 25 – see also Meek, p. 20).

10 *Transmigration:* this is still an Ibo belief. 'It is said that a bad man may be reborn as an animal, and an animal as a man. A man may also be reincarnated as a tree. In cursing another, then, an Ibo may sometimes express the hope that the other will be reborn not as a human being, but as a tree or a wild beast, or as an *okpango* or ape-like being.' (Meek, pp. 54–55).

10 *Ancestors:* a description of the cult of the ancestors amongst the Ibos can be found in Meek pp. 61–79.

12 *Swearing:* these expressions are similar to those in current use: 'may your body rot' (*rɛ kaa urɛ*), 'may your stomach swell' (*afɔ zaa ghi* or *otolo gbagbuɛ*), and 'may a leopard eat you' (*agɵ tagbuo ghi*).

12 *Purification:* Meek describes the ritual cleansing after an Ibo funeral as follows: 'After the inhumation all who have taken part enter a stream and bathe. Then, facing the direction from which the stream comes, they throw some water over their right shoulder. They face the direction

in which the stream goes, and do likewise. The intention is that the stream shall carry away the pollution of death.' (Meek, p. 308). The failure of the English to cleanse themselves in this way worried Equiano when he first arrived in England. (See p. 40.)

Customs concerning the supposed impurity of menstruous women vary, but a titled man like Equiano's father would 'avoid going near a menstruous woman, or eating food cooked by her'. (Meek, p. 275n.)

13 *Ah-affoe-way-cah:* the modern word for 'year' is *afɔ*. But there is no expression like 'ah-affoe-way-cah' in modern Ibo; these wise men would be called *dibia*. All the same, the expression may well be authentic, since in addition to the word *afɔ* it contains the word *ka*, which can mean 'to fix a date' (for festivals).

13 *Burials:* great men are customarily, though not invariably, buried in their homes, and Chinua Achebe writes that 'medicine men who were likely to prove troublesome after death would most probably be buried in the communal burial bush'. The return to the village by a different route may have been to avoid the spirits which would follow the path of the corpse to its grave.

13 *Physicians:* it is still common among the Ibo to treat swellings of various kinds by blood-letting. Hugh Crow records an instance of it at the end of the 18th century: 'The Eboes were very subject to headache and in order to relieve them we sometimes resorted to cupping. They were not strangers to the operation but told us it was a remedy often had recourse to in their own country.' (Crow, *Memoirs*, p. 227.)

13 *Running with the corpse:* this appears to have been common to many parts of West Africa, and the West Indies. Equiano refers to a description of a similar instance recorded in Lieut. John Matthews' *A Voyage to the River Sierra Leone*, London, 1788, pp. 121–124, and goes on to describe yet another, which occurred in the West Indies, as follows: 'An instance of this kind happened at Montserrat, in the West Indies, in the year 1763. I then belonged to the *Charming Sally*, Capt. Doran. The Chief Mate, Mr Mansfield, and some of the crew being one day on shore, were present at the burying of a poisoned negro girl. Though they had often heard of the circumstance of the running in such cases, and had even seen it, they imagined it to be

a trick of the corpse bearers. The mate therefore desired two of the sailors to take up the coffin, and carry it to the grave. The sailors, who were all of the same opinion, readily obeyed, but they had scarcely raised it to their shoulders before they began to run furiously about, quite unable to direct themselves, till at last, without intention, they came to the hut of him who had poisoned the girl. The coffin then immediately fell from their shoulders against the hut and damaged part of the wall. The owner of the hut was taken into custody on this and confessed the poisoning. I give this story as it was related by the mate and crew on their return to the ship. The credit which is due to it I leave to the reader.'

A description of a similar incident, this time in Ghana, will be found in the short story by Francis Selormey called *The Witch* (see Paul Edwards, *West African Narrative*, Nelson, 1963, pp. 150–164).

13 *Fear of poison:* an Ibo host will customarily taste the food and drink offered to guest, particularly if they are strangers.

14 *Snakes:* certain snakes, particularly the python (εκε) are reverenced amongst the Ibo, and the 'harmless snake' here was more likely to be a python than the 'crowing snake' (*ubi*), which is poisonous. I do not know how the story of the crowing snake originated, but it is still a widely held Ibo belief.

Chapter Two

15 *Emblems:* it is common Ibo practice to decorate the body with patterns in dye.

19 *Quotation:* I have not been able to trace this excellent couplet, which looks as if it should come from Pope's translations of Homer, but doesn't.

20 *To the left of the sun's rising:* presumably Equiano means to his own left, with his back to the sun, as he must at this point have begun to travel southwards. I don't think we can take this account of his journey to the coast too seriously. It is unlikely that the details would have remained clearly in his memory after over thirty years, particularly in view of the circumstances under which the journey was made. However, his coming to a great river is one thing

which he would be likely to remember, and it seems probable that this was either the Niger or one of the Delta rivers.
The tribe living in boats who spoke a different language
and terrified him so much might have been Ijaw, but I
think they were more likely Ibibio. Certainly the Ibos
of this time were very much afraid of them, and they bear
a certain resemblance, according to early records, to the
people described by Equiano. Adams wrote of them: 'To
this nation the Heebos express a very strong aversion and
call them cannibals. They certainly have a ferocious aspect
. . . they have very black skins and their teeth filed so as
to resemble a saw.' (pp. 40-41). Crow also described the
Ibibios north of Bonny – the Creek-men as he calls them:
'When they attain the age of seven or eight years their teeth
are sharpened with a file, and they do not hesitate to
acknowledge that they devour each other when occasion
offers. They live almost constantly in their canoes, in
creeks and corners, and procure a precarious subsistence
by marauding and plundering.' (p. 143). The picture of
the Ibibios is generally bad, but we should remember that
they were disliked by slave traders because they were less
tractable than the Ibos, and also that both Adams and
Crow probably got most of their information about the
Ibibios from Ibo informants. It seems most likely that
Equiano was taken to Bonny, though there is a possibility
that he might have gone to the other main slave port, Old
Calabar, down the Cross River – if the latter were the case,
it could be that Tinmah is the modern Utuma, since this
is approximately where Ibo ends and Ibibio begins, but
this seems unlikely as it would place Equiano's home much
too far to the east.

Adams has also left us an account of the last stages of the
journey of slaves to Bonny, which appears to resemble
closely Equiano's own experience. Adams writes: 'Fairs,
where the slaves of the Heebo nation are obtained, are
held every five or six weeks at several villages, which are
situated on the banks of rivers and creeks of the interior,
and to which the traders of Bonny resort to purchase them.
. . . Large canoes, capable of carrying 120 persons are
launched and stored for the voyage. . . . At the expiration
of the sixth day they generally return, bringing with them
1,500 or 2,000 slaves, who are sold to Europeans the evening

after their arrival, and taken on board the ships.' (pp. 38–39.)

20 *different countries . . . large woods:* second and later editions read: 'Through many dreary wastes and dismal woods, amidst the hideous roarings of wild beasts.'

20 *Languages:* when Equiano says that they did not totally differ, he is probably speaking of the different dialects of Ibo. There would have been Ibos all the way down to the coast along the slave routes, which explains why he 'always found somebody that understood him'.

Shells: these would be cowries. The figure he gives for the price paid for him, 172 cowries, seems much too small to be correct. More plausible might be 172 lbs. The price of a slave in lbs. of cowries fluctuated considerably, but it never dropped below 100 lbs. or rose above 300 lbs. during the eighteenth century, so far as I know. (See E. Donnon, *Documents Illustrative of the History of the Slave Trade to America,* Washington D.C., 1931, Vol. II, p. 28 and p. 309).

23 *The uncircumcised:* a contemptuous expression used by the Jews of other races.

23 *Scars:* it is odd that Equiano should express such a dislike of scarring the face, since this was widespread among the Ibos, and he records that his own father bore facial scars. It would have been a terrifying experience for a small boy, however, to have had these people offer to scar his face for him, and this might have been the origin of his dislike. But it may have developed after his arrival in England for he says later 'as I was now amongst a people who had not their faces scarred, like some of the African nations where I had been, I was glad I did not let them ornament me in that manner when I was with them'. (p. 40.)

24 *Six or seven months:* if he was turned eleven when captured (see p. 15) he would by this time have been nearly twelve, yet he speaks of himself as being 'near twelve years of age' on his arrival in England about a year later (see p. 39). It looks as if he did not know his exact age and the figures here must be taken as approximations within a year.

Chapter Three

30 *Quadrant:* an instrument of navigation for measuring the

angle of the sun, and consisting mainly of a graduated 90° arc.

31 *Parcels:* groups.

31 *Made us jump:* in order to find out which of them were the most active and healthy.

Chapter Four

34 *The African snow:* the snow was a small sailing vessel, much used in the slave trade.

35 *Thirty or forty pound:* this was a fairly high price to pay for an 11-year-old boy, and in 1753 the cost of a Gold Coast slave, valued higher than one from Calabar, was L.28 to L.30. But price fluctuated considerably, and at about the time Equiano was purchased by Captain Pascal (early 1757) they appear to have been higher than usual. One Captain claimed in November 1756 to have sold his cargo of slaves for L.40 to L.50 a head, and this price might have been forced even higher by the French attacks on slavers off the Gambia coast late in 1756, which probably resulted in a shortage of slaves. (See E. Donnan, *Documents Illustrative of the History of the Slave Trade to America*, Washington, 1931, Vol. II, pp. 507–513).

35 *Gustavus Vasa:* the original Gustavus Vasa (1496–1560) was one of the greatest of the Swedish kings. Equiano sometimes spells his name 'Vassa', for example in the title page of the book.

36 *Long passage:* we are told on p. 38 that it took 13 weeks, an exceptionally slow voyage. On p. 120 Equiano records a similar voyage as taking only seven weeks, and this appears to have been about normal. Capt. John Newton's three voyages, made between 1751 and 1754, each took between 48 and 55 days. (*The Journal of a Slave Trader*, ed. B. Martin E. Spurrell, Epworth Press 1962, see pp. 58–62, 82 and 94.)

36 *A native of America:* Dick would still have been a British subject since the Declaration of American Independence was not made until twenty years later, in 1776.

37 *Archipelago:* the Greek islands.

37 *Grampus:* a whale.

39 *Twelve years of age:* see the note above, to *Six or seven months,* p. 24.

40 *I had a great curiosity to talk to the books:* Equiano seems to
have taken this episode from an earlier book by another
African living in Britain, James Albert Ukawsaw Gronniosaw. The relevant paragraph in Gronniosaw's book,
published about 1770, is as follows:
'[My master] used to read prayers in public to the ship's
crew every Sabbath day, and when I first saw him read, I
was never so surprised in my life, as when I saw the book
talk to my master, for I thought it odd, as I observed him
to look upon it and move his lips. – I wished it would do so
to me. As soon as my master had done reading, I followed
him to the place where he put the book, being mightily
delighted with it, and when nobody saw me, I opened it,
and put my ear down close upon it in great hopes it would
say something to me; but was very sorry and greatly disappointed when I found it would not speak, this thought
immediately presented itself to me, that everybody and
everything despised me because I was black.' *A Narrative
of the most remarkable particulars in the Life of James Albert
Ukawsaw Gronniosaw* (Bath 1770? pp. 16.–17).
    The verbal similarities indicate that Equiano was using
Gronniosaw here, which suggests that some of the details
of his book might have been drawn not directly from his
own experience, but from those of his fellow Africans in
Britain. But this particular story about listening to the
books seems to have had something of the status of folk-
lore amongst the Africans in England at this time. It occurs
again in a slightly different form in the book, *Thoughts and
Sentiments*, by Equiano's friend Ottobah Cugoano (see p.
80: 'The Inca opened it eagerly, and turning over the
leaves lifted it to his ear. This, says he, is silent; it tells me
nothing; and threw it with disdain to the ground.')

41 *The Nore:* the district round Sheerness near the mouth of
the Thames, constantly used as an anchorage by the Navy
in times of war during this period.

Press gang: the law allowed captains of naval vessels to
41 'impress' men into service on their ships in time of emergency. Gangs of sailors from these ships would often search
other ships, or towns, using force to compel civilians to serve
in the Navy.

Chapter Five

43 *It was now two or three years:* in the previous year, Equiano had been with Capt. Pascal on the campaign of General Wolfe and Admiral Boscawen against the French in Canada. This expedition had sailed in February 1758, and later that year Boscawen returned, to take up a new appointment as Commander-in-Chief of the British force in the Mediterranean. It would have been just about two years after Equiano arrived in England for the first time, that he set sail with the Mediterranean fleet on the campaign which this chapter describes.

44 *The Miss Guerins:* sisters of a friend of Captain Pascal.

44 *Guide to the Indians:* this was a book called *The Knowledge and Practice of Christianity made Easy for the Meanest Mental Capacities: or, an Essay towards an Instruction for the Indians,* published in 1740 and written by Thomas Wilson, Bishop of Sodor and Man from 1697 until 1755. It consists of a series of imaginary dialogues between an Indian and a missionary.

44 *Rendezvous house:* a naval rendezvous ashore was a place where officers would gather to receive orders while their ships were in harbour.

44 *Watermen's wherries:* light rowing boats used to ferry goods and passengers on rivers.

46 *Levant:* the eastern Mediterranean.

46 *Bending their sails – shipping their cables:* raising their sails and taking their ropes aboard.

46 *Gunwale . . . main topmast head:* the gunwale is the barrier surrounding the deck, and the main topmast head is the top of the highest mast – thus the statement means 'from bottom to top'.

47 *Quotation:* the lines come from Pope's translation of Homer's *Iliad,* but are inaccurately quoted. The lines read:
    'Oh king! oh father! hear my humble prayer . . .
    If Greece must perish, we thy will obey,
    But let us perish in the face of day. (XVII ll.728-732)

47 *Monsieur La Clue:* Admiral de la Clue Sabran, commander of the French fleet during this campaign.

49 *Mizzen-mast:* the rear mast of a three-masted sailing ship.

49 *Main yard:* the yards or yard-arms are the cross beams which support the sail on the mast. This would be the yard

supporting the main-sail, which would be on the main-mast.

49 *A fire ship:* a ship filled with combustible materials, to be set on fire and sailed amongst enemy ships in battle.

50 *Havana:* the fleet sailed for Cuba under Admiral Pocock and captured Havana from the Spanish in 1762.

50 *The King died:* George II died in 1760.

51 *Cutwater:* the forward edge of the ship.

52 *Combings:* the raised sides of the hatches.

52 *Grappling irons:* naval warfare at this time often involved boarding an enemy ship while at sea. Grappling irons were used to grip the enemy ship and hold it close while it was being boarded.

52 *Rigging:* the masts and sails, and the ropes used to raise and lower them.

54 *Quotation:* from Milton's *Paradise Lost*, I. l. 175.

55 *Carcases:* missiles made of an iron shell with three holes, and filled with burning materials. Equiano could hardly have counted sixty of these in the air at the same time, and he probably means that he estimated this number.

Chapter Six

56 *Rule of Three:* elementary calculation, in which a fourth number is found from three given numbers, the unknown being proportionate to the third as the second is to the first.

57 *Messed:* had meals.

57 *I was as free as himself* etc.: in 1729, Yorke and Talbot, the Law Officers of the British Crown, gave a decision that a slave coming to Britain was not automatically free, as had sometimes been claimed, but this decision was constantly disputed by the anti-slavery movement. Granville Sharp, the leader of the movement, quoted the opinion of Lord Chief Justice Holt that every slave entering Britain became free, and acted on this belief on behalf of Jonathan Strong in 1765 and James Somerset in 1772. The latter was one of the most famous cases in the history of the abolition of slavery, for Lord Justice Mansfield declared in favour of the slaves, and from that time onward the Mansfield Decision was more or less accepted as law. But in Equiano's case here, the date was 1762-3 and the matter was still in doubt.

58 *West Indiamen:* ships sailing to the West Indies.
58 *Prize money:* shares in the value of captured ships and their
   cargoes shared between members of the crew of the captor.
62 *Quotation:* Thomas Day, *The Dying Negro*, published in
   1773. Equiano adds the following note to his quotation:
   'Perhaps it may not be impertinent here to add that this
   elegant and pathetic little poem was occasioned, as appears
   by the advertisement prefixed to it, by the following incident. "A black, who a few days before had run away from
   his master and got himself christened with intent to marry
   a white woman, his fellow servant, being taken and sent
   on board a ship in the Thames, took an opportunity of
   shooting himself through the head."'
62 *Quotation:* Milton, *Paradise Lost*, I. ll. 65–68.

Chapter Seven

65 *Gauging:* measuring.
65 *Droggers:* West Indian coasting vessels.
66 *King's Bench:* the King's Bench Prison, where debtors were
   jailed.
68 *Coopers:* makers and repairers of barrels.
68 *Stripes:* lashes with a whip.
69 *Quotation:* Milton, *Paradise Lost*, II. ll. 616–618.
71 *A Samoyed or a Hottentot:* two primitive peoples, the Samo-
   yeds being a mongol tribe from Siberia, the Hottentots
   aboriginal natives of South Africa.
71 *Mr James Tobin:* a member of the Council of Nevis, and
   author of *Cursory Remarks etc.* (London 1785), in which he
   defended the slave owners and attacked Ramsay's *Essay on
   the Treatment and Conversion of African Slaves in the Sugar
   Colonies* (London 1784). Cugoano attacks him as 'the Cursory Remarker' in *Thoughts and Sentiments*, p. 14. 'Zealous
   labourer' here is meant ironically.
74 *Quotation:* Milton, *Paradise Lost* II. ll. 332–340. The lines
   are slightly misquoted.

Chapter Eight

76 *Got the boat stove:* damaged the boat by splitting the hull.
78 *Geneva:* gin.

78 *Bits:* small coins, fractions of the Spanish silver dollar.

81 *Predestinarian:* one who believes life to be controlled by powers outside himself, so that he cannot determine the course of his own life. The events of his life are thus pre-destined by the gods or fate. This is still a widespread belief in West Africa, and is studied in M. Fortes' *Oedipus and Job in West African Religion*, Cambridge U.P., 1959. For another example of Equiano's fatalism, see his statement on p. 49, 'there was a time allotted for me to die as well as to be born . . .'

84 *Served his time:* completed his apprenticeship.

89 *Puncheon . . . hogshead:* types of large barrel.

Chapter Nine

92 *Rev. Mr George Whitefield:* a follower of John Wesley, Whitefield lived from 1714 to 1770, and gained a reputa-tion as the most impressive orator of the Methodist move-ment. Equiano must have been mistaken either about the preaching or the date, however, as Whitefield was at this time in England.

95 *Forty pounds:* the certificate of manumission shows that King was paid seventy pounds, not forty, for giving Equiano his freedom (see 1789 edition II. 18). This probably reflects the difference in value of the local currency from the pound sterling.

95 *He was pleased to promise me my freedom:* Mr King's reluctance to give Equiano his freedom may seem surprising in a Quaker. Since 1761, five years earlier, all Quakers were to be excluded from their Society if they continued to take any part in the slave trade. But since this had to be confirmed by further resolutions passed between 1774 and 1776, it seems that, like Mr King, not all Quakers were eager to obey the rules of their faith.

96 *The Apostle Peter:* Acts xii, verse 9.

100 *Yea-ma-chra:* the old Indian name for Savannah, on the coast of Georgia in the United States. The name appears to have survived as that of a suburb of the town. The name Savannah was given the town by Oglethorpe, the leader of the first settlement, but 'before his arrival in the country, it had the name of an Indian nation, viz. Yammacraw, who

inhabited there . . .' (John Harris: *Travels*, London, 1764, Vol. II, p. 326.)

103 *To work a traverse:* to tack a ship, i.e. to travel against the wind by taking a zigzag path.

Chapter Ten

106 *Lee-beam:* the side of a ship away from the direction of the wind.

109 *Dutch Creole:* the word Creole is normally used at this time for a white person born and living in a tropical colony. But this man is clearly distinguished from the white men, who did nothing to save their lives, and is presumably a mulatto.

113 *Hoy:* a small sailing boat.

116 *Dr Perkins:* a man who had had Equiano beaten unconscious in an earlier episode (not included in these selections) which took place in Savannah, Georgia.

Chapter Eleven

121 *Cherry Garden Stairs:* A landing place on the Thames about $1\frac{1}{2}$ miles below London Bridge.

123 *Dr Charles Irving's water freshener:* this was used with great success on the Phipps Expedition to the Arctic, on which Equiano travelled, described in Chapter Twelve. The following report was made on its efficiency by Captain Phipps in his *Journal:* 'We began this day to make use of Doctor Irving's apparatus for distilling fresh water from the sea: repeated trials gave us the most satisfactory proofs if its utility: the water produced from it was perfectly free from salt, and wholesome, being used for boiling the ship's provisions: which convenience would alone be a desirable object in all voyages, independent of the benefit of so useful a resource in case of distress for water. The quantity produced every day varied from accidental circumstances, but was generally from thirty-four to forty gallons . . .' (C. J. Phipps, *A Journal of a Voyage towards the North Pole 1773*, London, 1774, p. 28.) See also Phipps, *op. cit.*, pp. 205–221 for an account of how it worked.

126 *Franks:* the name was used of all European Christians in the Levant, originating during the Crusades in which the French played a major part.

126 *Inquisition:* the body of the Roman Catholic church concerned with the discovery and punishment of heresy. The Catholic Church holds that the Bible should only be put in the hands of those qualified to read it, and though the Bible is venerated, it is argued, Jesus 'refers those who were to embrace His doctrine, not to a book, but to the living voice of His Apostles and His Church . . . The Popes have warned Catholics against Protestant Bible Societies which distribute versions (mostly corrupt versions) of the Bible with the avowed purpose of perverting simple Catholics.' Catholics should read the scriptures only 'if they possess the necessary dispositions'. (W. E. Addis and T. Arnold, *A Catholic Dictionary*, London, 7th edition, 1905, pp. 87-89.)

127 *Garden of Eden, Oporto:* there are no records of a garden in Oporto of this name. There are, however, many fine gardens in the city, and one of these was presumably given this name by Equiano or his friends.

127 *Galley slaves:* galleys were ships driven by large numbers of oars, rowed by condemned criminals. Even after these had generally given place to sailing vessels, the Mediterranean powers continued to use them.

128 *Locust beans:* the name is applied in the Middle East to the bean from the pod of the Carob tree, since it was thought to resemble the insect.

131 *Assemblies:* these assemblies were well known, but not always spoken of so favourably. One informant from Jamaica recorded in the *Report on the Slave Trade* (1789) that 'Numbers of the negro slaves in that island perish or are rendered invalids by fevers, fluxes and pleurisies, occasioned by their habit of rambling to what are called *Negro Plays* or nocturnal assemblies, in distant parts, where they dance immoderately, drink to excess, sleep on the damp gound in open air, and commit such acts of sensuality and intemperance, as bring on the most fatal distempers'. (Part III, Jamaica, reply to Q. 11.) They were banned by the 1788 Jamaican Slave Act.

Chapter Twelve

132 *An expedition etc.:* the expedition led by Constantine Phipps in 1773, sought, like many previous expeditions, a sea route to the East Indies by way of the Arctic. The expedition sailed north to the island of Spitsbergen, and as Equiano says, reached a point further north than had any earlier explorers, though it beat Hudson's record, set nearly 200 years before, by only 25 miles. Nelson was a midshipman on this expedition. There are two other accounts of the journey. Phipps wrote his *A Journal of a Voyage towards the North Pole, 1773* which was published in 1774 and is the official record of the exact course taken by the ships. More entertaining is the account also entitled *Journal of a Voyage . . . towards the North Pole* by Commodore Phipps and Captain Lutwidge, also published in 1774. The hunting of bears and walruses mentioned by Equiano are there described in grotesque and comic detail (see for instance the bear-hunt, Phipps and Lutwidge, pp. 60-62).

133 *Sea-horses:* walruses.

134 *Some of our people etc.:* Equiano used the account by Phipps here, as there are several close verbal parallels between the two texts. For example, Phipps writes: 'At six in the morning the officers returned from the island; in their way back they had fired at, and wounded a sea-horse which dived immediately, and brought with it a number of others. They all joined in an attack upon the boat, wrested an oar from one of the men, and were with difficulty prevented from staving or oversetting her; but a boat from the *Carcass* joining ours, they dispersed.' (C. J. Phipps, *op. cit.*, pp. 57-58). According to Southey's *Life of Nelson*, ch. I, Nelson was in charge of the boat from the *Carcass*.

137 *Booms:* wooden spars stretching out at the base of the sail.

137 *Long-boat:* the largest of the boats carried aboard a sailing ship, used as a ferry between the ship and the shore when in harbour.

137 *Chucks:* wedges, holding a boat upright and firm when out of the water.

138 *Orfordness:* to the north of the mouth of the Thames estuary on the coast of Suffolk.

Chapter Thirteen

After the journey to the Arctic, Equiano describes, in the full text, how he made a study of several different religions and sects, and after a great deal of heart-searching was 'received into church-fellowship at Westminster Chapel', a centre of Calvinist-Methodist worship.

139 *Musquito Shore:* the name is a corruption of that of the Indian tribe living in Honduras and Nicaragua, the Miskito, and is usually spelt yet another way, as Mosquito. This tribe was traditionally friendly with the British, who established settlements in the region early in the seventeenth century, aided by the Indians themselves and the Dutch buccaneer, Captain William Bluefield (Wilhelm Blauveldt), both of whom were mortal enemies of the Spaniards who had colonized the mainland of South America. Mosquitia, as the region was called, might have become a British colony, since the Indians themselves wished it. They mobilized forces to help fight the Spaniards, loaned troops to help put down rebellion in the British islands, and sent their princes to be educated in British schools. The King of Mosquitia received his authority to rule from the Governor of Jamaica. But somehow, though troops and missionaries were resident there until late into the nineteenth century, Mosquitia never became a British colony.

140 *Fox's Martyrology with cuts: The Acts and Monuments of the Church, or Book of Martyrs* by John Fox (1517-1587), which was available in a number of abridged editions.

142 *Dupeupy:* detailed maps of this sparsely populated stretch of the Honduras coast show no settlement of this name, so it probably no longer exists.

142 *Cape Gracias a Dios:* this point was given its name by Columbus. It is told that he had promised his crew, on his fourth voyage of discovery, that if he did not sight land within three more days he would turn back. The cape was sighted, and Columbus declared 'gracias a dios', 'thanks be to God', after which the cape was named.

142 *Black River:* Rio Negro, in the east of Honduras.

142 *Guarda Costa:* the Spanish ships which policed the coastline of the Spanish possessions to guard against raiders and smugglers.

143 *Rum and pepper:* alcohol is widely recommended as a cure
for snakebite. The belief is mistaken, however, as its only
value would be to soothe the nerves of the victim, and it
might do harm by stimulating the circulation of the blood,
and so increasing the speed at which the snake-venom was
absorbed. The doctor's patients, it seems, recovered in
spite of his efforts.

143 *Woolwow or flatheaded Indians:* these are often referred to
by eighteenth-century travellers as Woolvas and are the
modern Ulua Indians, neighbours of the Miskitos. A number of Indian tribes, among them the chief tribes of the
Caribbean Islands, the Caribs and the Arawaks, practised
the distortion of the head in infancy by binding it. The
flattening of the brow which resulted was much admired.

143 *Silk grass:* a grass with a silk-like lustre from which fibres
were obtained.

145 *Life of Columbus:* this occurred during the fourth voyage of
Columbus, when the Indians of Jamaica, angered by the
pillaging of his sailors, refused to provide supplies. Columbus happened to know, from a book he had on board with
him, that an eclipse of the moon was due, so he summoned
the leading Indians and told them that God was angry with
them, and that they would be punished with famine. The
warning was to be the moon's losing its light. As soon as
the eclipse began the terrified Indians begged him to plead
with his God for mercy, and offered him all the provisions
he wanted. He retired to his cabin until the eclipse had
begun to pass, and then came out to tell the Indians he had
interceded successfully.

146 *Dryckbot:* Equiano's explanation of this odd word is not
very convincing. It may have been borrowed from the
Danes, who were active traders in the Caribbean and held
several islands at this time, and it might be rooted in some
such word as the Danish *drikkebord,* a drinks table.

146 *Casades:* cassava.

Chapter Fourteen

150 *One of St Paul's Men:* probably a reference to St Paul's
Epistle to the Galatians, 3, 28, which in the New English
Bible translation reads: 'There is no such thing as . . .

slave and freeman . . . for you are all one in Jesus Christ'
or to *Philemon*, 11–20, where Paul sends back a slave,
Onesimus, to his master, asking for him to be received
'no longer as a slave, but as more than a slave – as a dear
brother'.

But 'St Paul's men' was also a name given to the tricksters
who used to gather at St Paul's in London, and may imply
here someone who uses christianity for his own dishonest
ends.

152 *Tacking*: see note on 'to work a traverse' (p. 193).

154 *Manatee*: the sea-cow, a water mammal related to, and
slightly resembling, the dolphin.

156 *Dr Irving*: the Doctor had travelled to Jamaica at the same
time, but on '*The Squirrel*'.

157 'Granville Sharp, Esq; the Reverend Thomas Clarkson;
the Reverend James Ramsay; our approved friends, men
of virtue, are an honour to their country, ornamental to
human nature, happy in themselves, and benefactors to
mankind!' (Equiano's note)

158 *A system of commerce*: Equiano's ideas of trade were not
entirely new. Similar arguments against the slave trade
and in favour of increased commerce with Africa can be
found earlier in the 18th century (see, for example,
Malachy Postlethwayt, *Britain's Commercial Interest Explained and Improved*, London, 1757, vol. ii, pp. 215–220).
Equiano would have found quotations relevant to his ideas
about the economic future of Africa in one of the Appen-
dices to Benezet's *Some Historical Account of Guinea*, which
he acknowledges to have been one of his sources (see note
to p. 1). In the 1788 edition of Benezet, Postlethwayt's
Universal Dictionary of Trade and Commerce is quoted at some
length, arguing along similar lines to Equiano. Equiano
also put his case for trade with Africa in a letter to Lord
Hawkesbury, which was included in the *Report of . . . the
Privy Council* on the slave-trade, published in 1789 (see
Part I No. 14).

Appendix I

167 *Triumph*: see the Public Advertiser, July 14, 1787.